Year 1

Storybook Maths

Elaine Bennett
and Jenny Critcher

Acknowledgements

We are grateful for the contributions of the many people who have made this book possible and shared our enthusiasm for developing maths through stories.

Our thanks to:

The staff at Earls Hall Infant School who provided constant support, encouragement, friendship and who were always happy to try new ideas with us.

Mrs Helen Foster, an inspiring headteacher, who always encouraged us to be better practitioners and follow our ambitions.

The maths network we were involved with who were always interested to hear our ideas and gave us the confidence to begin working on ideas for these publications.

Judith Puddick at Southend-on-Sea LA for her advice and words of wisdom!

Carole Skinner and the team at BEAM for always championing our vision for making maths interesting, exciting and relevant for children, teachers and parents.

A very special thanks to the children at Earls Hall Infant School for making us want to write these books and making our job so worthwhile.

Finally, the most important thanks goes to our families, especially our wonderful better halves, Peter and Steve, who have been there for us throughout the whole process, sharing our excitement, giving us time and support when we needed it the most ... and to little Maxwell, who sometimes went to bed early so we could get on with our writing late into the night! And to Teresa Critcher for giving us the idea of even taking our ideas up to BEAM ... without that little push, it would never have happened.

Our sincerest thanks to you all!

Thanks to the children at Oakridge Parochial School, Gloucestershire, and Earls Hall Infant School, Southend-on-Sea, for their work.

Thanks also to the BEAM Development Group:

Joanne Barrett and Tina Bolton, Rotherfield Primary School, Islington
Catherine Horton, St Jude and St Paul's, Islington
Simone de Juan, Prior Weston Primary School, Islington
Sarah Kennedy, Highgate Primary School, Haringey

BEAM Education
Nelson Thornes
Delta Place
27 Bath Road
Cheltenham
GL53 7TH

Telephone 01242 267287
Fax 01242 253695
www.beam.co.uk
Enquiries cservices@nelsonthornes.com
Orders orders@nelsonthornes.com

© BEAM Education 2009,
   a division of Nelson Thornes

ISBN 978 1 9070 3402 2

British Library Cataloguing-in-Publication Data
Data available

Edited by Marion Dill
Design and layout by Reena Kataria
Cover illustrations: Nilesh Mistry
All other illustrations: Matt Carr

Photos: © GrantlyLynch.co.uk
Additional photos: Fran Mosley; Reena Kataria; Rotherfield Primary School, Islington

Printed and bound in Great Britain by Berforts Group

Contents

Introduction

Why Storybook Maths?

As dedicated infant practitioners, we have used stories daily in our teaching across the age range from the Early Years to the end of Key Stage 1. We have seen young children demonstrate delight and interest as they become familiar with, and grow to love, stories and the characters in them. This was the inspiration behind our idea to use stories as a vehicle for teaching maths and other areas of the curriculum.

When trying to find resources to support this approach, the only books we could find offered a limited number of activities that did not span the whole maths curriculum or age range. In some books, maths was not even mentioned, while links to subjects such as literacy and history were plentiful. This inspired us to develop resources to use within our school.

Our belief is that children learn and develop their mathematical knowledge and skills most successfully when provided with practical, engaging, real-life contexts. These can make maths something they feel involved in and excited about. Teaching maths through stories provides a natural way to embed 'using and applying', giving children a wealth of opportunities to consolidate and apply their understanding. Less confident children find stories a non-threatening way into learning. In addition, traditional tales can provide reassurance to children who are already familiar with the context.

We now know the importance of developing children's speaking and listening skills as part of their maths learning. Stories provide an ideal vehicle for talk as well as developing confidence with mathematical vocabulary.

Benefiting our VIPs!

The main aim of all practitioners is to nurture and inspire the 30 or so little VIPs in our classrooms. We aim to make our children feel positive about maths and believe that it is real and relevant to them. With storybooks as a focus, children work with a purpose and are motivated to learn. How much more exciting is it to weigh the contents of Red Riding Hood's baskets than classroom scissors and pencils!

Because children can relate to stories at their own level, stories provide teachers with opportunities for differentiation. Children also feel empowered to make decisions about their own learning. If maths is allowed to extend beyond a one-hour session, children have the time to explore and develop problem-solving strategies and approaches.

The bigger picture

There is nothing better than joining in children's excitement about what they are learning. Over the past few years, we have shared many special moments with each other and support staff when children have become immersed in the imaginative world of stories and totally enthralled with their learning in maths. The excitement of going to a 'school fair' (in the classroom), where children spend their money on stalls such as 'Hook a duck', 'Toy sale' and 'Coconut shy', resulted in children telling their parents in loud voices "I haven't done any work; we've played all day!" when, in fact, we knew they had been using and applying their mathematical understanding and taking some real steps in learning.

Maths through stories has become a whole-school approach, with each year group using stories that link to current topics while ensuring coverage of the curriculum.

Making links with parents is important if children are to reach their full potential. If you let parents know which stories are going to be used in maths teaching, they can share these stories at home with their children, either reading from books or retelling familiar tales. Parents are often not sure of how to support maths at home. Reading and telling these stories at home will remind children of the exciting activities that they have done that day or week. As children talk about what they have been doing at school, they help their parents see how to support their child's maths learning.

Getting started

- The activities in this book are not intended to provide a scheme of work to be followed; nor are they an exhaustive list. They offer an enjoyable and exciting collection of ideas to be shared, added to and dipped into with colleagues.

- It has taken time for stories to become embedded into the maths curriculum in our school. A good way for you to start would be to choose one story from the book, select one or more activities you like the sound of and dip your toe in the water.

- A bolder alternative is to start with a 'storybook maths week', where each class or year group focuses on one book for a week, working across the curriculum, but with a maths focus. We have done this in our school, and it was a great success: staff, children, parents and governors all had fun!

- In maths, there will always be skills that you need to teach directly. Once you have introduced them, children can develop their confidence in the skills, consolidating and applying them through work on stories.

- Above all ... enjoy!

How to use this book

This book has seven sections, all following the same format: three relate to modern stories and four to traditional ones. Each section offers ideas for activities on all the seven strands of maths, but focuses in particular on one of these strands:

- Using and applying mathematics
- Counting and understanding number
- Knowing and using number facts
- Calculating
- Understanding shape
- Measuring
- Handling data

Each story suggests links with possible topics, which you may find useful in your planning. For example, if you are going to do some work on healthy eating, *Handa's Surprise* is a good story to use and, mathematically, would give you opportunities to work on handling data. If you have work planned on farming and food, then consider introducing *The Little Red Hen* and do some work on knowing and using number facts.

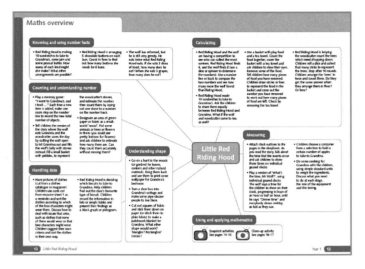

The maths overview outlines ideas for activities on six strands of maths and suggestions for taking some of the maths outdoors.

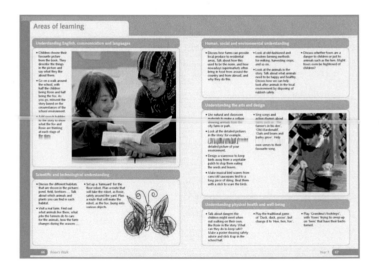

This section outlines opportunities for learning in other areas of the curriculum. There are brief suggestions for activities in:

- Understanding English, communication and languages
- Scientific and technological understanding
- Human, social and environmental understanding
- Understanding the arts and design
- Understanding physical health and well-being

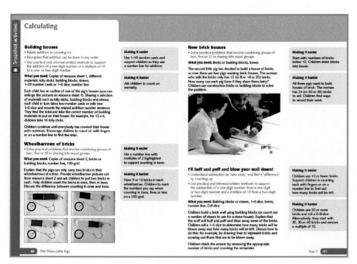

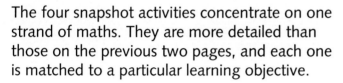

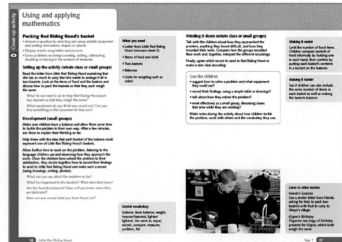

The four snapshot activities concentrate on one strand of maths. They are more detailed than those on the previous two pages, and each one is matched to a particular learning objective.

The close-up activity offers a detailed lesson plan, focussing on the same strands of maths as the snapshot activities. There are also ideas for differentiating the activity for children working at different levels.

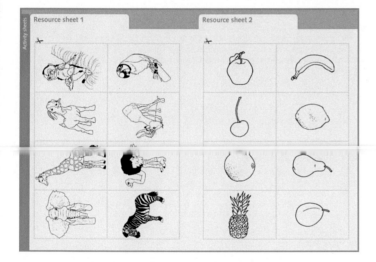

Each chapter contains two resource sheets. These are not worksheets, but contain templates for cards and props that we have found ourselves making numerous times over the years, and which we refer to in the activities earlier in the chapter.

You can adapt the sheets in various ways by enlarging, reducing or amending as necessary.

How to use this book

The close-up activity focuses on the same strand of maths as the snapshot activities.

Resources you need to carry out the activity

Links to EYFS/mathematics framework. The activity may cover several aspects of maths, but the main objective addressed is given here.

You can do the activity with the whole class or introduce it to a group at a time. We illustrate one way you can start off the activity, but you can adapt it as you see fit. We suggest a few things for you to say during this initial phase, to draw out children's explanations and to help them clarify their thinking.

Maths vocabulary that you might want to use in talking with children about their work

Close-up activity

Measuring

Party hats

• Estimate, measure and compare objects, choosing and using suitable uniform non-standard units and measuring instruments

Setting up the activity (whole class on carpet)

The animals are going to a hat shop to buy party hats for Kipper's party.

Show children your party hat. Try it on the animals, discuss which ones it fits and establish the idea that different animals need different-sized hats. Talk about real hat shops where grown-ups go, and where hats are marked with different sizes. Give each pair some paper strips of various lengths and establish a method of making a hat for their animal by sticking the ends together with no overlap.

Development (pairs and whole class)

Children measure their strips of paper with cubes or other units and write approximately how many units long it is on each one, then turn it into a hat. They decorate the hats and put them in the 'hat shop' (designate a place for this, such as a low table).

Do the cubes need to be close together or spaced out when you measure?

Is that hat a good fit? Or is it too loose/tight?

How could you tell or show someone else what you have done?

Winding it down (whole class)

As a class, take each animal to the shop in turn. The shopkeeper asks the animal if they know their hat size and helps them find a hat to fit. The shopkeeper records the size (in units) by the animal's name so that next time they come to the shop, they will know what size of hat to look for.

When all the animals are fitted out, look at the records and discuss the activity.

Do you think the koala needs a big hat? What size do you estimate that it needs?

If there is no hat size 12 to fit the duck, what can we do about it?

How many hats did we make in size 10?

Which animals needed the largest hat? The smallest hat?

What you need

• Stuffed animals of various sizes

• A simple party hat, based on a thick band of paper to fit around the head

• Paper strips of varying lengths

• Sticky tape

• Linking cubes, short sticks or square tiles

• Materials for decorating hats

Useful vocabulary

explain, compare, measure, unit, length, size, long, short, longer/longest, shorter/shortest, large, small, how many?

76 Kipper's Birthday

As with the setting-up section, here you find suggestions about how to develop and wind down the session as well as what to say when discussing the activity with children to draw them out mathematically.

Adapt the activity to children working at different levels by making it easier or harder.

Making it easier

Have strips of suitable lengths prepared, but do not measure with units. Children find a strip to match each teddy and turn them into hats. Talk about the length of the strips and whether any are too long or too short.

Making it harder

Show children how to use a ruler to measure the strips of paper to the nearest centimetre.

What did you find easy and hard about the task?
Would you do anything differently next time?

Can the children
• measure accurately with non-standard but uniform units?
• recognise the benefit of using uniform units as opposed to, for example, sticks of differing lengths?
• use mathematical language (longer than, shorter than, the same length as, close to, nearly) to compare the lengths of the strips directly?
• describe how they made the hats?

Make notes during the activity about how children tackle the problem, work with others and the vocabulary they use.

Links to other stories

Handa's Surprise
Children make headbands for themselves to support a basket like Handa has on her head.

Sleeping Beauty
Children make and decorate cone-shaped fairy hats.

Other possible story contexts for this activity to achieve the same mathematical purpose

As children work, observe what they do and say in order to make on-the-spot assessments. The more you can note down in class, the more food for thought afterwards as you reflect on the children's work and their achievements.

Little Red Riding Hood

Using and applying mathematics

The first version of this popular tale about a little girl taking a basket of goodies to her ill grandmother appeared in Charles Perrault's story collection in 1697. On the way to her grandmother's, Red Riding Hood meets a wolf who plans to eat both her and her grandmother. The wolf races ahead and tries to trick the little girl by dressing up as Grandma in bed. Fortunately, Red Riding Hood escapes the wolf, and the story ends with everyone except the wolf living happily ever after.

This is a story to work with for its own merits, although you may want to introduce it as part of a focus on traditional tales. Alternatively, use the story as a stimulus when doing work on families.

Maths overview

Knowing and using number facts

- Red Riding Hood is making 10 sandwiches to take to Grandma's, some jam and some peanut butter. How many of each kind might she make? What other arrangements are possible?

- Red Riding Hood is arranging 5 chocolate buttons on each bun. Count in fives to find out how many buttons she needs for 6 buns.

- The wolf has reformed, but he is still very greedy. He eats twice what Red Riding Hood eats. If she eats 3 slices of toast, how many does he eat? When she eats 5 grapes, how many does he eat?

Counting and understanding number

- Play a memory game: "I went to Grandma's, and I took …" Each time a new item is added, make one more step on the number line to record the new total number of objects.

- Tell children the version of the story where the wolf eats Grandma and the woodcutter saves the day by cutting the wolf open to let Grandma out and fills the wolf's belly with stones instead. Fill a small basket with pebbles, to represent the woodcutter's stones, and estimate the number, then count them by laying out one stone to a number on the number track.

- Designate an area of green paper or fabric as a small-world 'wood'. Put some animals or trees or flowers in there (you could use pretty buttons for flowers) and ask children to estimate how many there are. Can they count them accurately without moving them?

Understanding shape

- Go on a hunt in the woods (or garden) for leaves, conkers and other natural materials. Bring them back and use them to print some wallpaper for Grandma's bedroom.

- Turn a shoe box into Grandma's cottage and make some pipe-cleaner people to live there.

- Cut out squares of fabric and stick them down on paper (or stitch them to plain fabric) to make a patchwork blanket for Grandma. What other shape would work? Triangles? Rectangles? Circles?

Handling data

- Have pictures of clothes (cut from a clothes catalogue or magazine). Children use cards cut from resource sheet 1 as a reminder and sort the clothes according to which of the four characters might wear them. Discuss how to deal with issues that arise, such as clothes that none of them would wear or that two characters might wear. Children suggest their own criteria and sort the clothes in their own way.

- Red Riding Hood is deciding which biscuits to take to Grandma. Help children find out the class's favourite type of biscuit. Children record the information in lists or simple tables and present their findings as a block graph or pictogram.

Calculating

- Red Riding Hood and the wolf are having a competition to see who can collect the most conkers. Red Riding Hood finds 6, and the wolf finds 8 (use a dice or spinner to determine the numbers). Use a number line or track to compare the two numbers and see how many more the wolf found than Riding Hood.

- Red Riding Hood made 10 sandwiches to take to Grandma's. Ask the children to share them equally between Red Riding Hood and Grandma. What if the wolf and woodcutter come to tea as well?

- Use a basket with play food and a tea towel. Count the food together, cover the basket with a tea towel and ask children to close their eyes. Remove some of the food. Tell children how many pieces of food you have removed. Children draw circles or lines to represent the food in the basket and cross out the number you have removed to work out how many pieces of food are left. Check by removing the tea towel.

- Red Riding Hood is helping the woodcutter count the trees which need chopping down. Children roll a dice and collect that many sticks to represent the trees. Stop after 10 rounds. Children arrange the 'trees' in twos and count them. Do they get the same answer when they arrange them in fives? Or tens?

Little Red Riding Hood

Measuring

- Attach clock outlines to the pages in the storybook. As you read the story, talk about the time that the events occur and ask children to show those times on individual geared clocks.

- Play a version of 'What's the time, Mr Wolf?', using individual geared clocks. The wolf says a time for the children to show on their clock, progressing in leaps of an hour or half an hour, until he says "Dinner time" and everybody shows midday as fast as they can.

- Children choose a container from a selection to hold a certain number of apples to take to Grandma.

- Do some cooking for Grandma with the children, using simple standard units to weigh the ingredients. Discuss what you need to do at each stage, the role of the equipment and the timing.

Using and applying mathematics

 Snapshot activities
See pages 14-15

 Close-up activity
See pages 16-17

Using and applying mathematics

Repeating patterns

• Describe simple patterns and relationships involving numbers

What you need: Copies of resource sheet 1

Children sit in a circle. Give wolf masks (made from resource sheet 1, enlarged as necessary) to every third child around half of the circle and ask children with masks to stand. Children describe the pattern and work out who will be the next wolf. Repeat the pattern around the circle. Discuss whether and why the pattern is disrupted when you get to the end (because the number of children is not a multiple of 3).

Continue by giving masks to every second or fourth child. Predict whether you will need more or fewer masks.

Planning a celebration for Grandma

• Describe a puzzle or problem, using numbers, practical materials and diagrams; use these to solve the problem and set the solution in the original context.

What you need: Role-play equipment

Put the children in charge of planning a celebration for Grandma. Ask questions to prompt their planning, such as: "How many sandwiches, cups, plates, knives and forks will you need for Red Riding Hood and Grandma?"; "If Mum and the woodcutter join them, how many will you need then?" Children use role-play equipment to investigate and make a list of all the things they need for the dinner.

Help children record the information in a simple table and encourage them to talk about how they solved the problem.

Making it easier

Start with simple AB patterns so that every other child is a 'wolf'. Get children to give out the masks, working out who will be the 'wolves'.

Making it harder

Ask children questions such as: "Will the tenth child be a wolf?"; "How many children will be wolves in our circle?" Children give out wolf masks following their own pattern.

Making it easier

Limit the celebration to only two people: Grandma and Red Riding Hood.

Making it harder

Extend the problem. The woodcutter is bringing his four children to the party. How many of each item will the children need?

Shopping for Grandma

• Solve problems involving counting, adding, subtracting, doubling or halving in the context of money

What you need: 1p and 10p coins

Red Riding Hood is going to the shops to buy things for Grandma. Help the children write a price list with items – medicine, tissues, grapes – priced from 1p to 10p.

Give each child 10 pennies to spend. Discuss what they buy; how many things they buy; whether they spend all of their money; what is the greatest/smallest number of items they could buy?

Move on to spending a 10p coin on only one item and how to give change. What might Red Riding Hood have bought that gave her 2p change?

```
┌─────────────────────────────────────────┐
│  chemist shop                            │
│                                          │
│  medicine                         10p    │
│  yellow pills                      7p    │
│  white pills                       8p    │
│  ointment                          5p    │
│  big box of tissues                4p    │
│  small box of tissues              9p    │
└─────────────────────────────────────────┘
```

Designing a board game

• Describe ways of solving puzzles and problems, explaining choices and decisions orally

What you need: Simple track board games

Look at and play one or two simple track board games, talking about how to set them up and how to play them.

Next, children design and make a board game using the setting of the story. Talk with them about the decisions they make: the board; the playing pieces; how to make moves; what rules to invent; how many players can play? …

Encourage children to play each other's games.

Using and applying mathematics

Packing Red Riding Hood's basket

- Answer a question by selecting and using suitable equipment and sorting information, shapes or objects
- Display results using tables and pictures
- Solve problems involving counting, adding, subtracting, doubling or halving in the context of measures

Setting up the activity (whole class or small groups)

Read the letter from Little Red Riding Hood explaining that she has so much to carry that she needs to arrange it all in two baskets. Look at the items of food and the baskets and discuss how to pack the baskets so that they each weigh the same.

What do we need to do to help Red Riding Hood pack two baskets so that they weigh the same?

What equipment do you think you could use? Can you find something in the classroom to help you?

Development (small groups)

Make sure children have a balance and allow them some time to tackle the problem in their own way. After a few minutes, ask them to explain their thinking so far.

Help them with the idea that each bucket of the balance could represent one of Little Red Riding Hood's baskets

Allow further time to work on the problem, listening to the language children use and observing how they approach the work. Once the children have solved the problem to their satisfaction, they decide together how to record their findings to send to Little Red Riding Hood and make such a record (using drawings, writing, photos).

What can you say about the problem so far?

What has happened to the buckets? What does that mean?

Are the buckets balanced? How will you know when they are balanced?

How can you record what you have found out?

What you need

- Letter from Little Red Riding Hood (resource sheet 2)
- Items of food and drink
- Two baskets
- Balances
- Units for weighing such as cubes

Useful vocabulary

balance, lever balance, weight, heavier/heaviest, lighter/lightest, the same as, equal, record, compare, measure, problem, list

Winding it down (whole class or small groups)

Talk with the children about how they approached the problem, anything they found difficult, and how they recorded their work. Compare how the groups recorded their work and, together, interpret the different recordings.

Finally, agree which record to send to Red Riding Hood or make a new class recording.

> ### Can the children
> - suggest how to solve a problem and what equipment they could use?
> - record their findings, using a simple table or drawings?
> - talk about how they solved the problem?
> - work effectively as a small group, discussing issues that arise while they are working?
>
> Make notes during the activity about how children tackle the problem, work with others and the vocabulary they use.

Making it easier

Limit the number of food items. Children compare baskets of food informally by holding one in each hand, then confirm by putting each basket's contents in a bucket on the balance.

Making it harder

See if children can also include the same number of items in each basket as well as making the baskets balance.

Links to other stories

Handa's Surprise
Use a similar letter from Handa asking for help to pack two baskets with fruit to carry to Akeyo's village.

Kipper's Birthday
Organise two bags of birthday presents for Kipper, which both weigh the same.

Areas of learning

Understanding English, communication and languages

- Write a list of things to take to Grandma, such as medicine, flowers, biscuits, grapes or home-made jam.

- Read instructions for making simple cakes or biscuits, then make them.

- In the role of Red Riding Hood, write a diary entry for the day she went to Grandma's.

- Talk about ways to care for someone who is ill. What would they have done if they were Red Riding Hood? What would they have put in their basket?

Outdoor opportunities

Set up a role-play area of Grandma's cottage and the wood. Enlarge the pictures on resource sheet 1 and cut them out to make masks.

For Grandma

cake
jigsaw puzzle
magazine
lemon barley drink
flowers

Scientific and technological understanding

- Make cakes and observe how the ingredients mix together. How do the cakes change when they are in the oven?

- Red Riding Hood sometimes walks to Grandma's in the dark. What is the best colour and material for her hood to ensure you can see her? Use a dark place or dark box to explore which colours and materials show up the best.

- It is raining when Red Riding Hood walks to Grandma's. Children design and make a hood, an umbrella or a basket covering to stop Red Riding Hood or her basket getting wet.

- Write 'sorry' letters from the wolf to Grandma or Red Riding Hood, using a word-processing program. Insert clip-art pictures to make the letter really beautiful.

- Take photographs of the area around the school to make a photo map. Compare this with Red Riding Hood's local area. Are there any similarities? What differences can children identify?

Human, social and environmental understanding

- The story is set long ago. Look at pictures of clothes that people used to wear at bedtime: nightcaps, shawls, long nightgowns … How are these things different to today's nightwear, and why?

- What did Grandma's house look like inside and outside? How would her house be different if she lived nowadays?

- Children draw the route they take from their house to a friend's or relative's house or to school.

Understanding the arts and design

- Paint pictures of different scenes in the story and sequence them to make a storyboard.

- Make a large collage of the wolf in Grandma's bed, using a variety of fabrics. Give her a patchwork bedspread.

- The children become Red Riding Hood or the woodcutter. They look in a mirror and use the image to paint a self-portrait. Add features such as a hat, hood, beard …

- Children design a moving character puppet from stiff paper or card, using paper fasteners to enable the puppet's legs, arms and head to move. They use a variety of materials to decorate their puppets.

- Children design a 'slider' of the wolf in Grandma's bed. Read some moving picture books together, looking at how a slider is used to make parts of the story appear or disappear. Using strips of card, children fold one strip of card in half and staple at the open end. Use a second strip of card to fold around the first which can slide up and down. Decorate the first strip with a picture of the wolf and the second strip as the quilt of Grandma's bed. Children can explore making the wolf appear and disappear by sliding the second strip up and down over the wolf.

- Sing songs about characters who are ill, such as 'Miss Polly had a dolly' or 'John Brown's baby'.

- Use instruments to build a sound picture of the wood: for example, choose 'light, sunny' music as Red Riding Hood starts her journey, but as she gets deeper into the wood, find ways to make darker sounds.

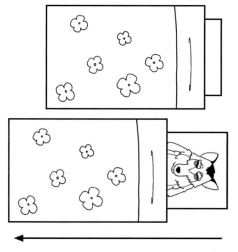

Understanding physical health and well-being

- Play a 'Grandma's cottage' relay game. Children run to a hoop filled with Grandma-style clothes, collect one item to bring back and give it to a volunteer 'wolf' to put on. The winning team is the first with a wolf dressed as Grandma.

- Play a simple version of tag rugby: children form into two teams, Red Riding Hoods and wolves. All the Red Riding Hoods tuck a band or ribbon into the back of their shorts.

The wolves have to move around the hall trying to remove their bands/ribbons. Have a time limit; the winners are the wolf who removes the most bands and any Red Riding Hood who has kept their band.

- Talk about why Red Riding Hood stopped to talk to the wolf in the woods, and whether it was wise of her to do so. When (if ever) should children speak to people they don't know? If never, why not?

- Discuss when we should take medicine and who should give it to us. Create class rules for keeping safe around medicines. Include a talk from the school nurse if possible.

- Make food to put in Grandma's basket: sandwiches or cakes. Talk about healthy and unhealthy options. Plan a healthy basket to take to Grandma.

Resource sheet 1

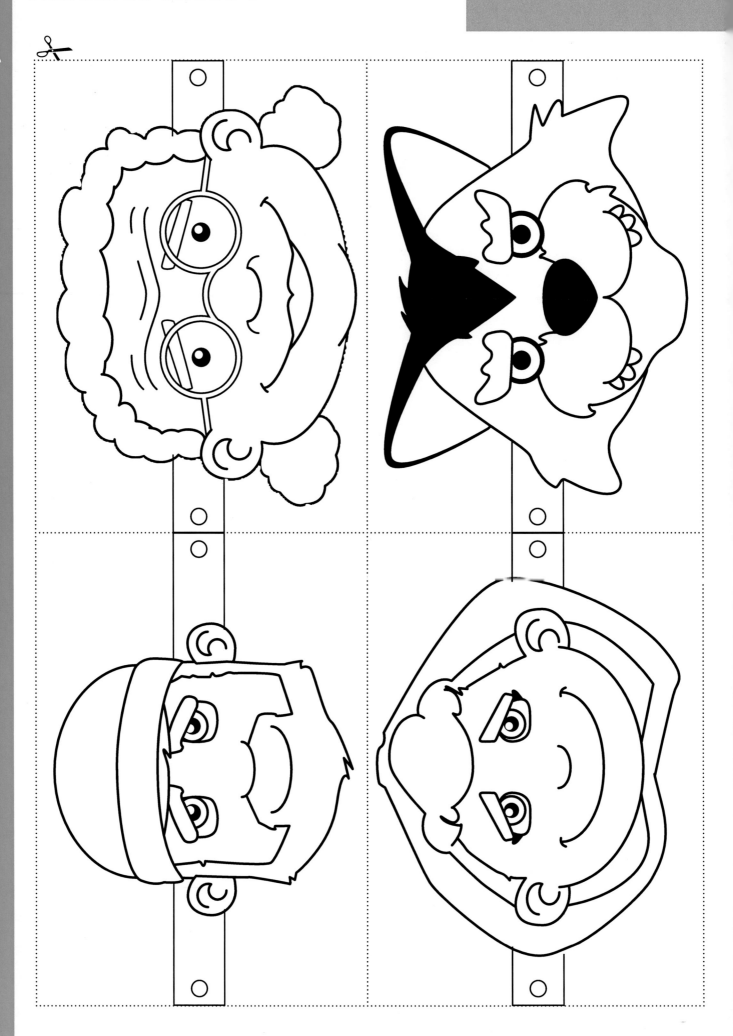

Fairytale Cottage
The Woods

Dear Class,

My name is Little Red Riding Hood.
I am writing to ask for your help. I am visiting
my Grandma, who is too ill to go shopping,
and I want to take her some food.
I have too many things to fit in one basket,
so I will carry two. The walk to Grandma's
is quite long, so I would like the baskets
to weigh the same.

Please will you send me your ideas
about how to pack them.

I hope you can help!

Love from

Little Red Riding Hood x

Sleeping Beauty

Sleeping Beauty

Counting and understanding number

Dating back to a 16th-century French tale, *Sleeping Beauty* is a story about a princess on whom a spell is cast shortly after her birth. On reaching young adulthood, she pricks her finger as predicted in the spell and falls asleep. She stays asleep for a hundred years until woken with a kiss by a handsome prince.

The story would fit in well with work on babies and naming ceremonies or other celebrations. It links perfectly with work on magic and magic beings. It also has a place in the topics of castles and other buildings.

Maths overview

Using and applying mathematics

- Are big presents always the heaviest? Use weighted boxes, wrapped up as presents, to find out.

- Provide blank tracks on paper cut into interesting shapes. Ask children to invent their own Sleeping Beauty board game.

Counting and understanding number

 Snapshot activities
See pages 26-27

 Close-up activity
See pages 28-29

Knowing and using number facts

- Give each child a strip of green paper for a stalk and 10 green triangles as thorns. Challenge them to find different ways of arranging the thorns along the stalk: for example, 3 on one side and 7 on the other. Record the number pairs

- Give children elf and fairy cards cut from resource sheet 1. Write numbers on the elves and fairies and put them in order to make number tracks, counting in ones, twos, fives or tens.

- Children repeat this spell: "Double, double, big bad trouble, make this number into a double." Pull a numeral from a 'feely' bag on the word 'double'. A pair of children each holds up that many fingers. Children count both sets of fingers to find out what the double is. They circle doubles on a number line and predict which numbers will never get circled.

Handling data

- Prepare pairs of dice, one with patterns on it (zigzag, spots, stripes, checked, hearts, wavy lines) and the other with colours (red, yellow, blue, red, yellow, blue). Give each child a copy of resource sheet 2. Children roll both dice and record the appropriate coloured pattern on each elf's or fairy's clothing. When you have plenty, cut out the cards and sort them on Venn diagrams, Carroll diagrams or tree charts.

- Everybody chooses an elf or a fairy from the cards made in the previous activity to go to the Sleeping Beauty's party. Use the cards to make a block chart showing the different kinds of pattern (or colour) on the guests' clothing.

Calculating

- Make up simple number stories about groups of elves and fairies coming to see the newborn princess. (Use play people or picture cards from resource sheet 1.) Record each story in a number sentence.

- The fairies travel to the castle in coaches. Each coach holds 2 (or 5 or 10) fairies. How many fairies would 2 (or 3 or 4 or 5) coaches hold? Record answers on a number grid and extend patterns.

- After their visit, 20 fairies need to get home. Five coaches arrive. Can children make sure each coach has the same number of fairies in it? Vary with other numbers.

- Children start with 10 (or 20) trees, cut from paper, in front of a castle outline. Roll a dice, say the number and, as the prince, cut down that many trees. Record the appropriate number sentence after each turn.

Measuring

- Talk about how many years the princess was asleep. Are years longer or shorter than months, weeks, days?

- Challenge the children to stay still like the Sleeping Beauty for a whole minute. Use a sand timer or a clock to measure the minute. Can they estimate when a minute has passed and wake up again?

- Draw alarm-clock faces on circles of card for Sleeping Beauty. Write the numbers to 12 in the correct positions and attach hands using paper fasteners. Set these alarm clocks to the time Sleeping Beauty should get up in the morning.

- Make towers using junk materials or construction equipment. Measure and compare the towers, using measuring tapes, cubes, paper strips, measuring sticks or rulers.

Sleeping Beauty

Understanding shape

- Make spiral (or helical) staircases. Draw or paint a spiral inside a circle and cut it out. Attach string to the top and hang up the staircases. Investigate, starting with different-sized circles.

- Children make a crown for the prince and decorate it with repeating patterns using sticky shapes, paint, or sequins.

- Children arrange themselves around the hall or play area, being prickly thornbushes. One child is Sleeping Beauty; another is the prince and closes their eyes. The other children give the prince directions to reach Sleeping Beauty, avoiding the thorns.

Outdoor opportunities

Draw the outline of a spiral on the ground, using chalk. How many steps does it take the prince to walk around it?

Counting and understanding number

How many fairies?

• Count reliably at least 20 objects, recognising that, when rearranged, the number of objects stays the same

What you need: Set of play people

Show the children a set of play people and explain that these are fairies in disguise. Count them together.

Talk about how fairies love to fly around. Say some magic words and make some of them 'fly', then say some more words to make the fairies land again. Ask the children how many they think there are now, then check.

Choose a child to say the magic words and rearrange the fairies again. Do children realise that the number stays the same? Can they say why it does?

Fairy cakes

• Use the vocabulary of halves and quarters in context

What you need: Paper circles, cards cut from resource sheet 1

Give each child a paper circle (fairy cake) and either 2 or 4 elf/fairy cards from resource sheet 1. Allow children time to try and work out a fair way of sharing the cake between the fairies/elves.

Encourage children to draw lines and, when they are confident about these, to cut along them. Bring the children back together and look at their pieces of cake. Get them to decide whether they have cut the cake fairly. If they decide that they did not, give out more paper circles and invite them to try again. Introduce vocabulary such as: *half, quarter, fair, equal, the same*.

Making it easier

Use only 3 to 5 play people. If children become confident with this number, move on to using more play people.

Making it harder

Use more play people. Before counting them, children estimate how many there are and record estimates on a number line.

Making it easier

Demonstrate how folding the circle in half can help.

Making it harder

Increase the number of elves/ fairies the cake needs to be shared between. Discuss what would be the most slices they could get from one cake. If the cake were bigger, would they get more slices?

Magic steps

- Compare and order numbers, using the related vocabulary
- Read numerals from 0 to 20, then beyond

What you need: Chalk or masking tape, numbered carpet tiles or circles; number line or track

Draw two parallel lines on the floor in chalk, 2 or 3 metres apart, to be the banks of a river (or use masking tape). Between these banks, spread out a set of 'stepping stones' (numbered carpet tiles or circles). Explain to a pair of children that the prince has to cross the river using stepping stones in order to reach the princess. These stones must be in the correct sequence.

One child (the prince) stands on one river bank, with 0 (or 1 or the first number in the sequence) in front of them. They step onto that, ask their partner to find the next number they need and put it in front of them. They cannot move until the number is there. They continue until they have crossed the river.

Building towers

- Compare and order numbers, using the related vocabulary
- Count reliably at least 20 objects

What you need: 1–6 dice for each child, dishes, trays of cubes; sticky notes, 0–9 dice, number line

Give each child a 1–6 dice, a dish and a tray of cubes. Give them one minute to roll their dice repeatedly, each time collecting the correct number of cubes to put in their dish. Children do not need to count the cubes after each addition, but just keep rolling and collecting.

After a minute, children stop and build Sleeping Beauty's tower with their cubes. Compare the various towers and establish which has most and which has fewest cubes.

Making it easier

Work with 5 stepping stones only. Pin up a number line or track to remind children about the order of numbers.

Making it harder

Allow just a few seconds before the step disappears and the prince falls into the water!

The stepping stones can show any consecutive sequence such as 21, 22, 23, 24 … or can be numbered in twos, fives or tens. Challenge children to make the next five stones for the sequence.

Making it easier

If towers topple over, make trains instead. When comparing them, make sure they are all lined up with their 'rears' against a base line.

Making it harder

Children work in pairs to roll a 0–9 dice and collect that many cubes, 10 times. They predict the total they expect to get and mark this on a number line. Discuss ways of counting the cubes accurately by arranging them in fives or tens. Mark the actual total on the number line and compare it with the estimate.

Counting and understanding number

Party guests

- Say the number that is 'one more' or 'one less' than any given number, and '10 more' or '10 less' for multiples of 10

Setting up the activity (whole class or small groups)

Set up a role-play scenario and explain that the King and Queen are getting ready to throw a party for their new baby and have invited lots of people. It is important that they know how many guests will be attending.

Show children the 100-grid, circle '5' and tell them that this is how many guests have accepted invitations so far. Just then, answer your phone and explain that the Royal Secretary on the other end is telling you that there is one more guest coming. Invite children to tell you the new number expected and to check by finding 'one more' on the 100-grid, using their 'wand'.

Receive a few more phone calls, finding 'one more' or 'one less' guest each time. Each time, children predict the number without looking at the 100-grid, then check on the grid.

Use the language of 'one more' and 'one less' and of addition and subtraction.

> *If one more person comes to the party, how many will there be? What number is 'one more' than 5?*

> *What is the number 'one less' than 8?*

Get to a total of 10 guests, then receive a phone call saying '10 more' guests are coming. Model 'adding on 10' by counting along in steps of one with your wand. Draw a circle around the answer.

Repeat the phone calls saying '10 more' guests are coming. Encourage children to predict the new number each time, checking by counting in steps of one on their 100-grid.

Sometimes have 10 guests cancelling and ask children to find the new number. Use the language of '10 more' and '10 less' and of addition and subtraction.

> *Ten more people are coming to the party. What is the total now? What number is '10 more' than 20?*

> *What is the number '10 less' than 60?*

What you need

- Demonstration 100-grid
- A telephone (real or pretend)
- Individual 100-grids
- Pencils with stars at the end (for wands)
- 1–10 number track or washing line

Useful vocabulary

predict, explain, count, more, less, fewer, add, total, altogether, subtract, take away, one, two, three ..., hundred, ones, tens

Development (small groups)

Pairs of children work together. One has a 100-grid and wand, and the other closes their eyes. Repeat the activity above: call out a starting number for the children to circle on their grids. 'Ring up' the pairs and tell them about one more acceptance or one more cancellation. The child with closed eyes predicts the new number, and the child with the wand checks on the grid.

After a few turns, children swap roles.

As before, children reach 10, then start adding or subtracting 10 guests per phone call.

Winding it down (whole class or small group)

The party is over. Exactly 100 guests came, but now they are going home in coaches which each hold 10 people.

Circle '100' on the grid. Children look away (or if you are using a grid on the whiteboard, hide the grid) and tell each other how many guests they think will be left after the first coachload has gone. They then look at the 100-grid to confirm the actual number.

Repeat this until all the guests have gone.

If we start at 100 and go back 10, what number do we get to?

We are on 80, and 10 more guests leave. What number is '10 less' than 80?

Can the children

- find the number 'one more' or 'one less' with the aid of the 100-grid?
- find the number 'one more' or 'one less' mentally?
- find the number '10 more' or '10 less' with the aid of the 100-grid?
- find the number '10 more' or '10 less' mentally?
- explain their methods?

Make notes during the activity about how children tackle the problem, work with others and the vocabulary they use.

Making it easier

Use a washing line or the number line from 1 to 10. Choose a number and tell the children that is how many guests are coming to the party. Use the wand to model how to work out the new numbers when 'one more' guest accepts or when a guest cancels.

Making it harder

Move on to finding the number 'one more' (or '10 more') or 'one less' (or '10 less') than various two-digit numbers: for example, 'one more' than 34 or 59 or '10 less' than 45.

Links to other stories

The Little Red Hen
Children keep track of the number of grains the hen has by finding 'one more' (or '10 more') or 'one less' (or '10 less') on a 100-grid.

Handa's Surprise
Children keep track of the number of fruits Handa has by finding 'one more' (or '10 more') or 'one less' (or '10 less') on a 100-grid.

Areas of learning

Understanding English, communication and languages

- Children write invitations to Sleeping Beauty's naming ceremony.
- Turn the role-play area into a castle.
- Children make a castle word wall, with related words displayed on the bricks.
- Children make up rhyming spells for the fairies.

- Children use small-world toys to act out the story.
- Talk about the bad fairy. Have children ever felt cross, left out or upset? What did they do?
- Talk about the gifts that the fairies gave to Sleeping Beauty. Were they toys? What would you give Sleeping Beauty?

Outdoor opportunities

Set up a quiet reading area inside a tent. Emphasise the need for quiet so as not to wake Sleeping Beauty.

Scientific and technological understanding

- Look at different plants with the children and discover which ones have thorns. What purpose might these thorns have? Look at how other living things protect themselves.

- Make a cress forest. When it has grown, cut it down like the prince cut down the thorny hedges in the story.

- Construct a forest using skittles as trees. Guide a programmable toy (with a picture of a prince on it) around the forest to reach the castle.

- Use a paint program to make pictures to illustrate the story.

- Look at how brick walls are built and use construction materials to build both weak and strong brick walls.

Outdoor opportunities

Build castles and towers outside, using construction toys, boxes or real bricks.

Human, social and environmental understanding

- Talk about how people change as they grow older. In the story, Sleeping Beauty starts as a baby; ask how the children have changed since they were babies. Talk about what they were able to do at each stage. Children then make a timeline of their lives so far.

- Think about when the story is set. Look at the picture of a spinning wheel and discuss what it was used for. Look at and talk about some new and some old household objects.

- Talk about Sleeping Beauty being a very old story. Encourage the children to ask their parents and grandparents which stories and nursery rhymes they enjoyed as children.

- Find some pictures of castles around the world. Discuss life in a castle. Look at the features of a castle such as drawbridge, moat, arrow slits, and what they are for.

- Talk to the children about how newborn babies are welcomed into the community and how different cultures celebrate their naming ceremonies.

> Dear Fairy Belinda
>
> we are having a party for our baby. Please will you come to our party?
>
> Love from the Queen

Understanding the arts and design

- Make a mural of the fairies visiting Sleeping Beauty. Each child contributes to it by making a fairy or an elf.

- Make Sleeping Beauty's or the prince's bedroom in a shoe box.

- Look at portraits of princes and princesses and talk about them. Children paint pictures of themselves as princes or princesses.

- Look at pictures of old castles, then visit an old building or, if possible, an old castle. Look at the stones or bricks used to build it. Do some stone or brick rubbings.

- Make puppets or masks to re-enact the story.

- Sing lullabies from a range of cultures and talk about how they help babies calm down and fall asleep.

- Use instruments to create some soft, soothing lullaby music and record this. Listen to the recordings.

Understanding physical health and well-being

- Play 'Musical statues'. The children run around, then freeze once a spell is cast (a bang on a tambourine). How long can they hold their frozen positions for?

- Think carefully about how the plants grew up around the castle. Express this in a simple dance.

- Talk about the importance of sleep. What would happen if we did not sleep? How long do we sleep for? Talk about the children's bedtimes and bedtime routines.

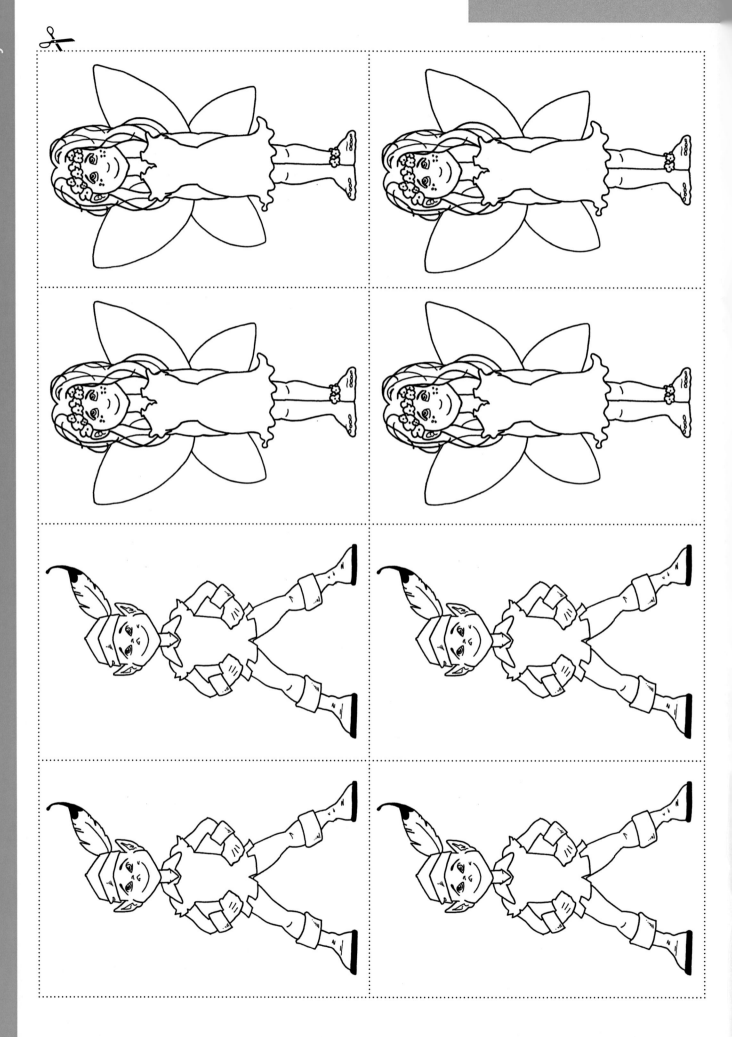

The Little Red Hen

The Little Red Hen

Knowing and using number facts

This traditional English folk tale, recorded for the first time in the late 19th century, features a hard-working hen and a bunch of lazy farmyard animals who are not willing to help her do the tasks necessary to grow wheat to make flour for bread. However, they are more than willing to help her eat it!

You can spend time working on this story in its own right or as part of a focus on traditional tales. Alternatively, use the story when working on farming and harvest, food, gardening or growth.

Maths overview

Using and applying mathematics

- Make up a price list for a baker's shop. Write a new list where all the items are increased by 1p (or reduced by 2p or doubled or halved).

- Provide children with a number track (straight, wiggly, zigzag, semicircular). Challenge them to make a board game based on the story. What good/bad things could happen along the way?

- Use cards cut from resource sheet 1 or 2 to make repeating patterns. Disrupt the pattern in some way and see if children can spot what has changed.

Counting and understanding number

- You need small-world animals and a 'farmyard' (a tray or sheet of card). Children roll a 1–3 dice and add that many animals to the farmyard or remove them. They aim to reach a target of exactly 10 animals.

- Each child scoops up a pot full of small-world animals. They count how many animals they have and check on a number line to see who has the most/least.

- Children cut up real bread rolls into halves and quarters and record how many pieces they get.

- Children roll a 1–3 dice and collect that number of 'grains of wheat' (yellow counters). Once they have 10 grains, they exchange them for a 'stalk of wheat' (a lolly stick with fringed paper to form the ears). The first person to get 2 stalks of wheat is the winner.

Knowing and using number facts

 Snapshot activities
See pages 38-39

 Close-up activity
See pages 40-41

Handling data

- Talk about the red hen's unhelpful friends. Children draw things people might do at home or at school in order to be helpful – or the opposite. Put two large hoops on the carpet, labelled with a smiley face (helpful) and a sad face (unhelpful). Work with the children to sort the pictures into the appropriate set.

Calculating

- Each child is an animal friend of the little red hen's. She has relented and decided to give them some of the rolls she made (that is, two cards from resource sheet 2). Children work out how many rolls they have altogether and write a number sentence to match.

- Make a price list for a bakery. Children choose two items to buy for the little red hen. They work out how much the total is by counting up on a number line. They then work out which coins to use.

- The little red hen has a purse with 5 pennies in it. Children take turns to roll a 1–6 dice and a dice showing ' + + + + − − '. They add pennies to the purse, or subtract them from the purse, according to the roll of the dice. Help them talk about what they are doing. After two turns each, children count the pennies in the purse and agree how to spend them at the bakery, using the price list made for the previous activity).

- The lazy farmyard animals have mended their ways and offer to help the little red hen sow her wheat. Share out a number of 'wheat seeds' (yellow counters) between the animals. Make sure the sharing is fair and count how many seeds each animal gets. Count any leftovers as well. At the end, sow the seeds (each 'animal' sticks down their seeds on a square of card).

The Little Red Hen

Measuring

- Make some bread with the children. Talk about how they measure the different ingredients and why measuring is important.

- Talk about the months of the year and the seasons. What does the hen do in the different seasons?

- Compare the weights of a range of real bread rolls, using a balance. Move on to predicting, then checking, how many cubes balance each roll.

Understanding shape

- Turn a floor robot into the little red hen and program it to travel to the places in the story. Talk about the position of the hen and the direction and distance she moves.

- Make windmills: attach paper sails to a card stick with a paper fastener. Put a spot on one sail and explore making quarter, half and full turns.

- Use biscuit cutters to cut shapes from sliced bread and talk about the shapes made and the shapes of the holes left in the slice.

Knowing and using number facts

Sharing bread rolls

• Derive and recall all pairs of numbers with a total of 10

What you need: 10 salt-dough bread rolls or paper circles

Make 10 small bread rolls out of salt dough or use brown circles of paper. Explain that the little red hen has decided to share her bread rolls with one of the other animals. If she shares them fairly, how many do they get each? And if she shares them unfairly?

Children find different ways of sharing the rolls and record these.

Doubling flour

• Recall the doubles of all numbers to at least 10

What you need: Cards cut from resource sheet 1

The little red hen can make two loaves of bread from one bag of flour. The amount of loaves is always double the amount of flour she uses. Children use cards cut from resource sheet 1 to model how many loaves they can make from different amounts of flour.

Children ask each other questions such as: "If the hen has 3 bags of flour, how many loaves can she make?"

Making it easier

Use only 5 rolls.

Making it harder

Expect children to find all the possibilities and to record systematically.

Making it easier

Support children in counting the bags of flour in ones and and the loaves in twos.

Making it harder

Work with doubles to 10 + 10 and beyond. Cover up the loaf cards and continue to ask questions: "If the hen has 5 bags of flour, how many loaves can she make?" Move on to covering the flour bags instead: "If the hen made 8 loaves, how many bags of flour did she use?"

Harvest number tracks

• Count on or back in ones, twos, fives and tens

What you need: Cards cut from resource sheet 1, strips of sugar paper; counters

Children stick cards cut from resource sheet 1 on long strips of sugar paper to make number tracks for counting in ones, twos, fives or tens. Help them record the number of flour bags, wheat stalks, and so on, under the tracks.

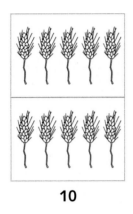 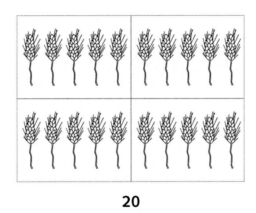

10   20

Making it easier

Stick to counting in ones and tens.

Making it harder

Children take turns to cover up one of the numbers on their track with a counter. Their partner has to work out the missing number.

Eating bread rolls

• Derive and recall addition facts for totals to at least 5
• Work out the corresponding subtraction facts

What you need: Cards cut from resource sheet 2, counters; 0–9 dice

Children take on the role of a hungry animal. They pick a card cut from resource sheet 2 and count the bread rolls. They take that many counters to represent these and decide how many to eat now and how many to keep till later. They record this in a way that makes sense to them. Talk to them about their recordings.

When the children have made several such recordings, ask them questions about the numbers: "The cat had 3 rolls, and she ate 2. How many did she keep till later?"

Making it easier

Support children with their recordings and talk to them about how to make them easy to 'read'.

Making it harder

Instead of using the cards from resource sheet 2, which limit numbers to 5, children roll a 0–9 dice.

Expect children to work out the answers to your questions quickly, using instant recall.

Knowing and using number facts

Doubling oven

• Recall the doubles of all numbers to at least 10

Setting up the activity (whole class or small groups)

The little red hen has a fairy godmother who has taken pity on her. To recompense her for her unhelpful friends, the godmother has given the hen a magic oven. However many loaves she puts in there, twice as many come out.

One child, the 'hen', rolls the 1–10 dice and counts out that many 'loaves' (counters) to put in her 'oven'. While the hen looks away, another child counts out the same number and puts those in the oven, too. Everybody counts to 20 to give the loaves time to cook before taking them out and counting them.

Children record the dice number and its double.

$$4 \longrightarrow 8$$

How many loaves do you think there are altogether now?

What kind of numbers are we getting with these doubles?

Development (teacher-led groups)

Pairs of children continue to roll the dice, and each child puts that many counters in their oven. They give the loaves time to cook, then remove them and count them. They record the dice number and its double.

If you doubled 4 and got 9, why would you know you had made a mistake?

What dice number did you get that gave you 12 loaves altogether?

What you need

• 1–10 dice or spinner

• Counters

• 'Magic' boxes to represent ovens

• 1–6 dice or spinner

• 1–20 dice or spinner

Useful vocabulary

explain, read, write, record, count, pattern, set, group, double, one, two, three, the same number as, as many as, equal to, add, makes, total, altogether

Winding it down (whole class or small group)

Work with the children to record the numbers from 1 to 10 in order, with their doubles.

$$1 \longrightarrow 2$$
$$2 \longrightarrow 4$$
$$3 \longrightarrow 6$$

Cover up any number and ask individual children to tell you what number you have hidden.

What do you notice about all the doubles numbers?

How do you know that double 5 cannot be 20?

> ### Can the children
> - work confidently, finding doubles of the dice numbers?
> - talk about their work and results?
> - remember doubles of numbers to 5? To 10? Beyond 10?
> - say what number must be doubled to give any even number to 10? To 20? Beyond 20?
>
> Make notes during the activity about how children tackle the problem, work with others and the vocabulary they use.

Making it easier

Use a 1–6 dice.

Making it harder

Use a spinner with numbers from 1 to 20.

Links to other stories

Sleeping Beauty
Children roll a dice to find out how many fairies are going to the party, wave a wand and double the number.

Handa's Surprise
Handa and her friend have two identical baskets. Children roll a dice to find out how many pieces of fruit to put into one basket and put the same amount into the other basket.

Areas of learning

Understanding English, communication and languages

- Write letters to the red hen from one of the friends, apologising for not helping her make the bread.

- Take photos of children helping in the classroom. Children write captions for the photos to be displayed.

- Read and compare different versions of the story. Do the same animals appear in all versions? Are there any significant differences between versions?

- Look at pictures of various animals and choose or invent words to describe their characteristics: scratchy cat, clucking hen, woofy dog.

Outdoor opportunities

Play some parachute games to develop cooperation. What happens if only one person moves the parachute?

Scientific and technological understanding

- Put some yeast in warm water with a bit of sugar and observe what happens. Go on to make bread. Observe the changes that happen as the bread bakes.

- Work with the children to grow fields of cress. Investigate what happens if the cress is not given sun or water or warmth. Does this tell the children about what the little red hen needs to do to keep her wheat growing healthily?

- Discuss how the wheat was cut by the little red hen and use scissors to cut the cress children have grown. Explore how scissors work, using movement around a pivot. Children can make model scissors using card and paper fasteners.

- Leave a small camera in the classroom so that children can take photos of their friends when they are being helpful.

- Create pictures from the story using a paint package and write captions for them.

Outdoor opportunities

Provide a digging area outside where children can sow grass or wheat seeds.

Human, social and environmental understanding

- Look at pictures of old farming equipment and talk about how it was used. Compare these to modern equivalents.
- Make a simple picture map of the farm in the story.
- Talk about the animals who lived on the farm with the hen. Those animals were lazy, but how do real farm animals help us?

- Talk about what the little red hen should do with the bread she made. Should she share it with her friends even though they did not help her?
- Make a 'helping wall' out of paper. Every time a child does something helpful, their name is added to the helping wall with a caption about how they have been helpful.

> Amy
> Tidying up
> the book case

> Ryan
> Finding the
> missing scissors

> Freddie
> Helping Findlay

Understanding the arts and design

- Mix up different yellows and browns in order to paint pictures of loaves of bread.
- Make play-dough loaves in various shapes and think up names for these shapes: cottage loaf, bun, house, wiggly snake …

- Explore the sounds of instruments. Which ones work well to accompany grinding grains? Mixing and kneading dough? Make shakers using beans/pulses/rice to imitate the sound of rain falling on the wheat field.

- Talk about musical tempo. The animals were lazy and slow. The hen was very busy. How could children show this with the instruments?
- Listen to slow and fast pieces of music: for example, Bach's 'Air on the G string' and Rimsky-Korsakov's 'Flight of the bumble bee'. How do children want to move when they hear them?

Understanding physical health and well-being

- Look at food groups and identify which one bread belongs in. Discuss how different groups contribute to a healthy diet.
- Discuss what the red hen might put on her bread: butter, peanut butter, jam … Identify the food groups these belong in.

- Discuss the levels of activity of the animals in the story. Would the children be healthy if they were as lazy as some of the animals?
- Set up apparatus in the hall to be different parts of the farm. Children take on different characters from the story and travel in role round the farm: slowly and lazily, quickly and busily …

Resource sheet 1

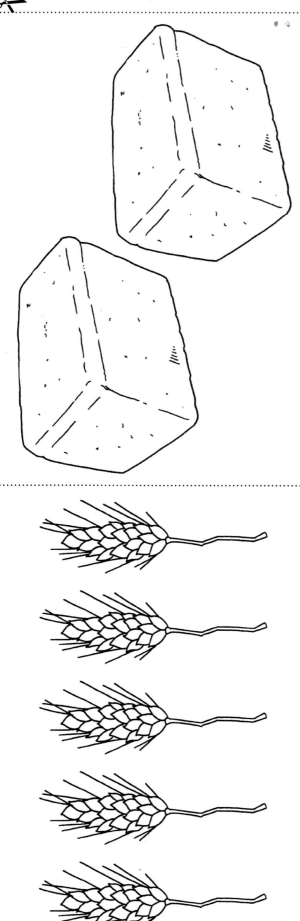

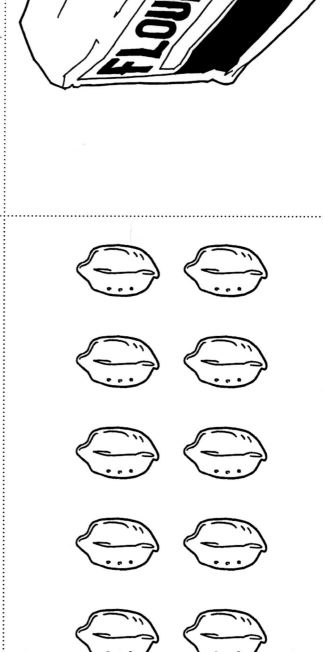

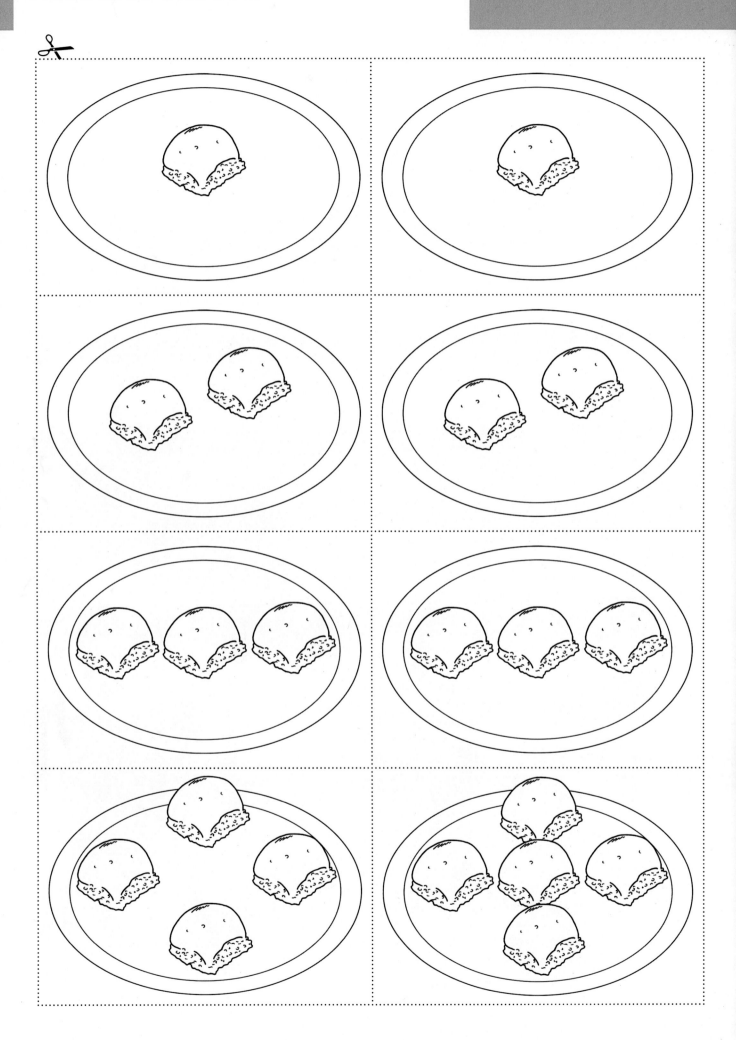

The Three Little Pigs

Calculating

One of the first-know versions of *The Three Little Pigs* dates back to an English fairy-tale collection from the late 19th century. The story is quite similar to a popular tale by the Brothers Grimm, *The Wolf and the Seven Young Kids*.

The three little pigs are building a house each out of a chosen material: straw, sticks and bricks. All is well until the wolf comes along and tries to blow down the houses. It is soon clear that the only safe house is the one made of bricks. The wolf, unable to blow down the brick house, climbs onto the roof with the intention of reaching the pigs by climbing down the chimney, but meets a sticky end when he falls into a pot of hot water.

Use the story in conjunction with other traditional tales or alone, to focus on the social aspects of houses and homes. It is also a useful starting point for work on the properties of materials and the building of structures.

Maths overview

Using and applying mathematics

- The third pig's bricks cost 8p. He needs one more to complete his house. What coins could he use to pay for the brick? How many different ways could he pay for it?

- Give children a toy pig and provide a selection of construction equipment, paper, sticky tape, and so on. Can they build a house for this pig? Talk with children about the choices they make. Extend to two or three pigs: will the house be big enough? How could they adapt it?

Counting and understanding number

- Children pick a number card from 10 to 20. They count out the correct number of building bricks and build a wall for the pig's house.

- Children pick a number card from 5 to 10 and build a wall with that number of bricks. They take turns to roll a '+/−' dice. If they roll a '+', they take one more brick for their wall; if they roll a '−', they return a brick. On each turn, children predict, then check, how many bricks they have.

- The pigs have decided to move into town. Use pictures of street houses cut from resource sheet 1, labelled with numbers to 10 or 20. Mix up the pictures and ask children to put the houses in the correct order. Remove some of the houses and ask children to work out which are missing.

Understanding shape

- Provide cards of building equipment cut from resource sheet 2 (two sets) and copies of a simple picture showing three shelves. Children play a barrier game. Child A places four or five pieces of equipment on their 'shelves' and describes to Child B where each item is. Child B uses these instructions to put the same items in the same places. Child A removes the barrier, and the pair checks the position of the items.

- Use a toy wolf and pictures of the pigs' houses cut from resource sheet 1. Make a simple grid map with the house pictures in three different squares. Child A gives the wolf directions to reach each house in turn, using the language of 'quarter' and 'half turns'. Child B moves the wolf accordingly.

- Children make house pictures using sticky shapes. Collect the pictures, choose one in secret and place a scrap of paper underneath. Identify the house to the children by describing the shapes used for details, such as windows or chimneys. Children work out which house you chose. When they are confident with the game, they can play in pairs.

Knowing and using number facts

- Bricks come in red and brown. The third pig uses 10 bricks altogether. How many of each brick type might he use? What other possibilities are there?

- At the builders' yard, they are having a 'Buy one, get one free' sale, which means they give you double the number of bricks you ask for. One child rolls a dice to see how many bricks to buy; another child counts out double that number of bricks. Together, they use the bricks to build a wall.

Measuring

- Children make houses for the pigs on different tables, then find out which is longest, which is tallest, which has the highest door … Children need to find a way to make these comparisons without moving the houses (as they might fall down).

- Children make a zigzag book of the story from the wolf's point of view, with one main event on each page, such as blowing down the first house. Children draw clock times for each event, using the language of 'o'clock' and 'half past'.

The Three Little Pigs

Calculating

 Snapshot activities
See pages 50-51

 Close-up activity
See pages 52-53

Outdoor opportunities

The pigs need a pot of water big enough to fit the wolf. Use a soft toy as the wolf and provide lots of containers. Which one will be most suitable for the pigs' needs? How much water can it hold?

To build a brick house, the third pig needs to use 'concrete' which is made of 1 litre of sand, ½ litre of water and ½ litre of gravel. Children measure out the materials and mix them together to make concrete.

Handling data

- Find out the different types of houses children live in. Decide how to collect the information (using a simple table or lists) and how to present the results (pictures, simple block graph or pictogram). Ask children simple questions about the data they have collected.

- Give children pictures of houses (bungalows, detached houses, semi-detached houses, flats). Children sort these using their own criteria. Ask them to re-sort the houses using given criteria such as number of storeys or windows.

Calculating

Building houses

- Relate addition to counting on
- Recognise that addition can be done in any order
- Use practical and informal written methods to support the addition of a one-digit number or a multiple of 10 to a one- or two-digit number

What you need: Copies of resource sheet 1, different materials: lolly sticks, building blocks, straws, 1–20 number cards or 1–6 dice; number line

Each child has an outline of one of the pig's houses (you can enlarge the pictures on resource sheet 1). Sharing a selection of materials such as lolly sticks, building blocks and straws, each child in turn takes two number cards or rolls two 1–6 dice and records the related addition number sentence. They find the total and take the correct number of building materials to put on their house: for example, for 12 + 4, children take 16 lolly sticks.

Children continue until everybody has covered their house with materials. Encourage children to count on with fingers or on a number line to find the total.

Wheelbarrows of bricks

- Solve practical problems that involve combining groups of two, five or 10 or sharing into equal groups

What you need: Copies of resource sheet 2, bricks or building blocks; number line, 100-grid

Explain that the pigs can only carry two bricks in their wheelbarrows at a time. Provide wheelbarrow pictures cut from resource sheet 2 and ask children to put two bricks in each. Help children count the bricks in ones, then in twos. Discuss the difference between counting in ones and twos.

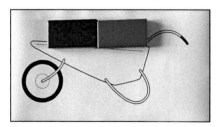
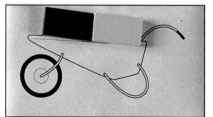
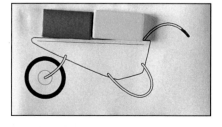
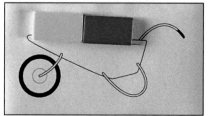

Making it easier

Use 1–10 number cards and support children as they use a number line for addition.

Making it harder

Ask children to count on mentally.

Making it easier

Use a number line with multiples of 2 highlighted to support counting in twos.

Making it harder

Have 5 or 10 bricks in each wheelbarrow. Children to mark the numbers you say when counting in twos, fives or tens on a 100-grid.

New brick houses

- Solve practical problems that involve combining groups of two, five or 10 or sharing into equal groups

What you need: Bricks or building blocks; boxes

The second little pig has decided to build a house of bricks, so now there are two pigs wanting brick houses. The woman who sells the bricks only has 12 (or 8 or 16 or 20) bricks. How many can each pig have if they share them fairly? Children use construction bricks or building blocks to solve the problem.

Making it easier

Start with numbers of bricks below 10. Children share blocks into boxes.

Making it harder

All three pigs want to build houses of brick. The woman has 24 (or 30 or 36) bricks to sell. Children find ways to record their work.

I'll huff and puff and blow your wall down!

- Understand subtraction as 'take away' and find a 'difference' by counting up
- Use practical and informal written methods to support the subtraction of a one-digit number from a one-digit or two-digit number and a multiple of 10 from a two-digit number

What you need: Building blocks or straws, 1–6 dice; bricks, number line, 0–9 dice

Children build a brick wall using building blocks (or count out a number of straws to use for a straw house). Explain that the wolf will huff and puff and blow away some of the bricks. Children roll a 1–6 dice to determine how many bricks will be blown away and how many bricks will be left. Discuss how to do this: for example, by drawing lines to represent bricks and crossing out those that are to be blown away.

Children check the answer by removing the appropriate number of bricks and counting the remainder.

Making it easier

Children use 10 or fewer bricks. Support children in counting back with fingers or on a number line to find out how many bricks will be left.

Making it harder

Children use 20 or more bricks and roll a 0–9 dice. Alternatively, they start with 20, 30 or 40 bricks and remove a multiple of 10.

Calculating

At the builders' yard

- Use the vocabulary related to addition and subtraction and symbols to describe and record addition and subtraction number sentences
- Relate addition to counting on
- Recognise that addition can be done in any order
- Use practical and informal written methods to support the addition of a one-digit number or a multiple of 10 to a one-digit or two-digit number

Setting up the activity (whole class or small group)

Set up a role-play builders' yard with the children's help. Display materials and tools (or pictures of these cut from resource sheet 2). Involve children in making a price list and pricing the actual objects, using sticky labels.

Development (small groups)

Tell the children they are animals planning a visit to the builders' yard to buy materials. Talk about what they will need and help them each choose two objects from the price list: for example, a bundle of sticks and a ladder.

Children list the objects they are going to buy on paper, using words or drawings, and write down the price for each item. Talk about strategies for finding the total of the prices: for example, counting on, using fingers, a number line or informal written methods …

Children find the total cost, recording this as a number sentence: for example $12p + 6p = 18p$. Model the language to use in discussing this.

How much does the ladder cost?

How much do your two things cost altogether?

Can you find the total cost? How might we do that? Is there anything you could use to help you?

Once children have found the total, they find coins to make up the correct amount. They then visit the builders' yard with their shopping lists to buy the items.

Can you find the coins for your total?

Can you use fewer coins to make your total?

What you need

- Role-play equipment for builders' yard: trowel, bricks, sticks, bags, hammer, ladder, rope, paintbrush, paint … (or cards cut from resource sheet 2)
- Clipboards and paper for price list and shopping lists
- Sticky labels
- Coins

Useful vocabulary

money, price, pay, coin, pence, change, cost, how much altogether?, total, add, count on, more than, equals, plus

Winding it down (whole class or small group)

Investigate pairs of items that 10p or 20p could buy at the builders' yard. Discuss the strategies children are using to find the totals of the prices.

Has anyone used number bonds or addition facts they know by heart?

What equipment can you use to help you do the addition?

Move on to finding the greatest number of items children could buy for 10p and 20p.

Suppose we bought lots of straw at 2p a bag. How many bags could we buy? How shall we work it out?

Can the children

- find the total of two prices?

- record a number sentence to represent adding the prices of two items?

- talk about the strategies they use to find the total of the prices?

- use coins of various values to make up amounts?

- show understanding of equivalent values?

Make notes during the activity about how children tackle the problem, work with others and the vocabulary they use.

Making it easier

Children choose one item from the shopping list to buy for their house. Give children pennies to pay for it. When the children are confident buying one item, ask them to buy two and put the number of pennies for each item into separate piles. Children then combine the number of pennies for each item and count how many there are altogether.

Making it harder

Investigate the different ways children can pay for their goods: what is the smallest amount of coins they could use? Once children are confident, extend the prices beyond £1. Explore pound and pence notation with the children and make new price labels for the items in the yard.

Have a new set of price tags: some with two-digit prices and some with prices up to 10p. Children add a one-digit price such as 8p to a two-digit price such as 23p. Introduce informal written methods: for example, drawing all the 10p coins and all the 1p coins, adding the 10p coins first, then adding on the 1p coins.

Links to other stories

Kipper's Birthday
Set up a party shop with items that Kipper could buy for his party.

Areas of learning

Understanding English, communication and languages

- Write an alternative story ending.

- Children write a letter from the wolf to the pigs, apologising for his behaviour.

- Role-play the story in small groups. Encourage children to work together, sustain their roles, evaluate performances and make contributions to the planning of the performance.

Scientific and technological understanding

- Discuss the materials the pigs chose for their houses. Which house would have been the strongest? Why? Groups build a small house for the pigs out of twigs, straw or building blocks. Test the strength of each house by blowing them with a hairdryer.

- Explore which roof materials would keep the pigs dry. Provide a selection of materials and test by dripping a specified amount of water onto each one.

- Explore real-life animal homes (wild and domesticated). Compare human homes (as the pigs have in the story) with pigsties and freerange pig huts, looking for similarities and differences.

- Use a word-processing program to write a 'Wanted' poster to warn other fairy-tale creatures about the wolf, detailing what he looks like and what he did wrong. Discuss the font, size and style of the writing needed for a poster.

- Use a video camera or still photography to record children's role play (see the third activity in *Understanding English, communication and languages*). Use these to evaluate performances and suggest improvements.

Outdoor opportunities

Set up a role-play builders' yard in the play area. Provide bricks, sticks, straw, wood, rope, guttering and other materials for children to experiment with.

Human, social and environmental understanding

- Talk about building houses today and in the past. What materials did people use? How were the houses constructed?

- Take a walk around the local area. Look at the construction of the houses and security measures people take to protect their homes.

- Find out about houses around the world. Talk about how the materials used and construction methods link to the local environment.

- Talk about the wolf's behaviour in the story. Have the children ever felt scared or threatened and how did they deal with the situation? How could the wolf make up for his behaviour at the end of the story?

- Should the pigs forgive the wolf for blowing down their houses? Discuss whether the children ever have had to forgive someone for something they have done. Is it an easy thing to do?

Understanding the arts and design

- Design a simple house for a different fairy-tale character: for example, Little Red Riding Hood. Children construct the house and design the interior, using paint, wallpaper or printing.

- Use printing or rubbing techniques to make brick walls as in the third pig's house.

- Retell the story using voices and instruments: for example, for 'huffing and puffing', children all blow together.

- Learn rhymes and songs about houses such as: 'This is the house that Jack built' or 'In a cottage in a wood'.

Outdoor opportunities

Pin up some large sheets of paper on a wall. Children use rollers and paint brushes to make wallpaper for the pigs' houses.

Understanding physical health and well-being

- Use skittles or cones to represent the pigs' houses. Children roll balls from different distances, trying to knock down the houses.

- Use benches or other equipment. Children pretend to be the wolf climbing up and jumping down to escape the pot of hot water.

Resource sheet 1

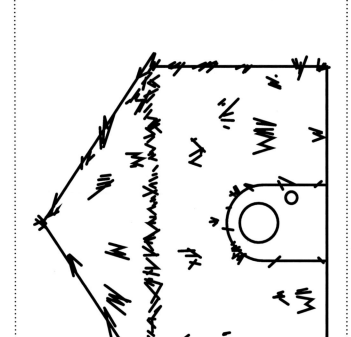

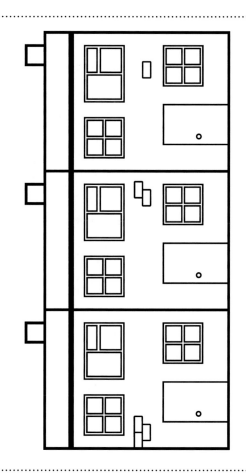

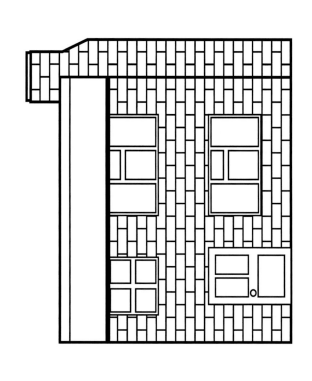

Resource sheet 2

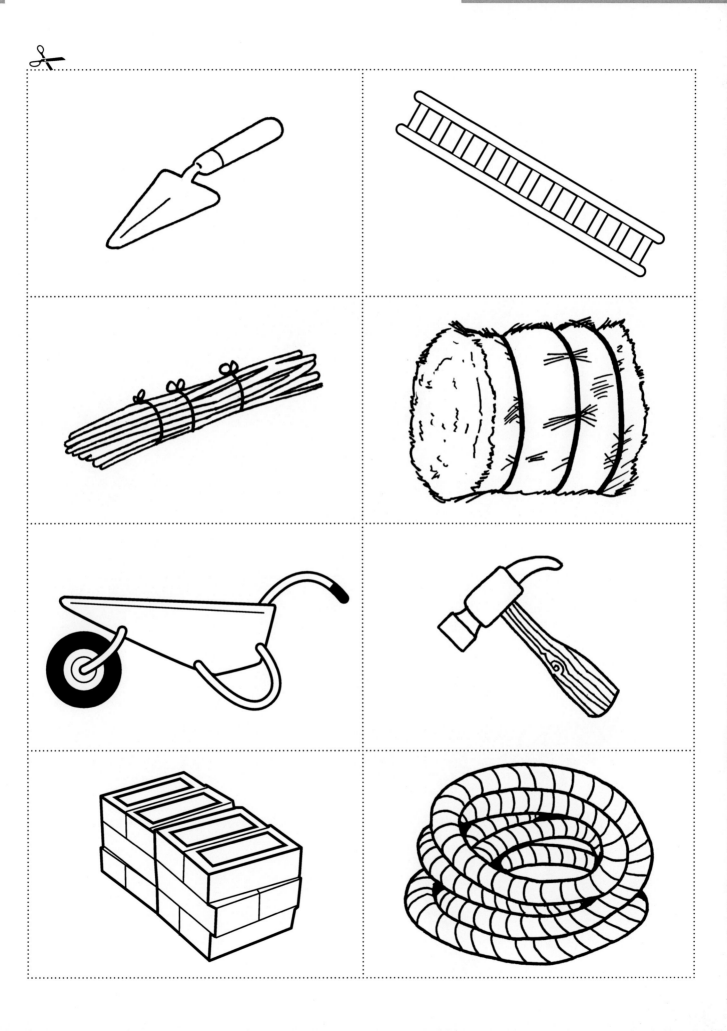

Rosie's Walk

Understanding shape

This picture book by Pat Hutchins, first published in the 1970s, has become a modern classic. Rosie, the hen, goes for a leisurely stroll around the farmyard, totally unaware of the hungry fox following her and of the accidents which prevent him from catching up with her.

This story would fit well with work on animals and farms, or journeys. It also links to work on safety.

Maths overview

Using and applying mathematics

- Cut out picture cards from resource sheet 2. Use these pictures to make a pattern such as beehive, bee, beehive, bee. Extend to AAB, ABC patterns. Set up some patterns with mistakes. Can the children spot these and correct them?

Counting and understanding number

- Each child has a piece of paper shaped like a beehive. They pick a number card from 5 to 10 and put that number of 'bees' (yellow counters) on their hive. They then take turns to roll a dice with '+ / −' on its faces. If they roll a '+', they take one more bee; if they roll a '−', they put one back. On each turn, children predict, then check, how many bees they have.

- In the book, look at the picture of a pear tree on the page where Rosie crosses the yard. Each child has a large outline of a tree and draws 10 pears on it. Pin or hang these up in a line and use them to practise counting in tens. Announce a multiple of 10 such as 50 and challenge children to tell you the number '10 more' or '10 less'.

- Instead of going around the pond, Rosie goes across the pond. The children work together to make stepping stones from paper, numbered from 1 to 10 or 20. When these are in the correct order, Rosie can cross safely. When they are in the wrong order, the fox (or whoever is crossing) falls into the water.

Handling data

- Talk about how bees make honey and hold a bread-and-honey tasting. Children rate how much they like it on a scale of 1 to 5. Record this on a bar chart.

- Look at the plants and minibeasts in the pictures. Sort small-world insects or real leaves and flowers and talk about how you have sorted them.

- Talk about what Rosie passes on her walk and what the children pass as they walk to school every day. What do most people pass? How could the children find out and record this?

Calculating

- Children have two sorting dishes and a 1–6 dice. They roll the dice and put that number of small-world farm animals in the first dish; they repeat this for the second dish. They find out the total number of animals and record this as a number sentence.

- Each child in a pair rolls a 1–10 dice and collects that many small-world animals. They arrange each set in a line and work out the difference between the two lines.

- Use 20 real or fabric leaves. Children work out how to share them fairly between the four branches of a tree drawn on paper and stick them down.

Measuring

- Rosie sets off at 10:00 am. Every half hour, she passes a landmark. Pin labels to the pages to show each time. Ask questions such as: "What time does Rosie pass the mill?"

Understanding shape

 Snapshot activities
See pages 62-63

 Close-up activity
See pages 64-65

Rosie's Walk

Knowing and using number facts

- Give each child 8 (or 5 or 7 or 10) 'pears' (green or yellow counters) and two tree outlines. Children find as many ways as they can to split the pears between the trees.

- In the story there are two mice. Roll a 1–10 dice and say the number. Take that many counters and decide what food item they represent. That is enough for one mouse. Double that to find how many food items two mice eat: for example, 6 grains of wheat ⟶ 12 grains of wheat. Find a way to record this.

Outdoor opportunities

Use posts and other PE equipment to represent landmarks from Rosie's walk. Work outside to plan where to put these landmarks, remembering that the first landmark, her house, is also the last one! Use a metre stick to measure approximate distances between the landmarks.

Understanding shape

Making a board game

- Visualise and use everyday language to describe the position of objects and direction and distance when moving them

What you need: Dice, counters, cards cut from resource sheets 1 and 2; circular track

Give children dice, counters and cards cut from resource sheets 1 and 2. Ask them to design a Rosie board game using some or all of this equipment. Leave children to discuss this for a few minutes, then join the discussion. Help them clarify their ideas and make suggestions as appropriate.

Encourage children to describe the rules of their game: clarify how many dice are used, how the players move around the board, and so on.

Making a communal map

- Visualise and use everyday language to describe the position of objects and direction and distance when moving them

What you need: Cards cut from resource sheet 2; cards cut from resource sheet 1, small-world objects, large sheet of paper

Children draw items from the story and cut these out. Work together, sitting round a large sheet of paper, to stick down the cards to make a big map of the farm. Discuss the route Rosie takes, emphasising that it is roughly circular.

As a group, retell the story as you move fox and hen cards cut from resource sheet 2 around the map.

Making it easier

Work with the children, using a circular track you have already prepared. Encourage them to dicuss possibilities and make decisions.

Making it harder

Challenge the children to include some simple calculations in their game: for example, they might add the numbers on two dice or write question cards which players pick up when they land on certain squares.

Making it easier

Children use cards cut from resource sheet 1 for the map and place them as you tell the story. They can add flowers, mice and frogs, and so on.

Making it harder

Use cards cut from resource sheet 1 and a grid drawn on paper. Give instructions about Rosie's journey: "She walks 2 squares forward and makes a half turn clockwise. She walks 3 squares forward and is at the beehive." Children stick down the beehive picture in the correct square.

Going round the farm

- Visualise and use everyday language to describe the position of objects and direction and distance when moving them

What you need: Enlarged cards cut from of resource sheet 1, PE apparatus

Set up PE apparatus in the hall, with enlarged pictures cut from resource sheet 1 stuck on, to represent the farm.

Give children some time to explore the stations. Children then take turns to give each other instructions for a different kind of walk round the farm: for example, "Go round the beehive twice. Now go to the pond and jump over it …" Focus on using and responding to a wide range of directional and positional language.

Windmills

- Identify objects that turn about a point (scissors) or about a line (a door)
- Recognise and make whole, half and quarter turns

What you need: Paper sails, card sticks, paper fasteners

Talk about how the cap of old-fashioned windmills rotated so that the sails could face the wind, wherever it came from. Tell a story about a windy day when the wind kept changing direction. Children pretend to be windmills and follow your instructions: the sails turn round to the left by a quarter turn, then to the right by a half turn. Do they all end up facing the same way?

Making it easier

Children work in pairs. One child gives instructions; the other one carries them out. Support the children giving instructions by suggesting ideas if necessary.

Making it harder

Include clockwise and anticlockwise turns and half or quarter turns left and right.

Making it easier

Stick to whole and half turns. Indicate the direction the mills should turn by pointing as well as using speech.

Making it harder

Make windmills: attach paper sails to a card stick with a paper fastener. Put a spot on one sail and explore making quarter, half and full turns with the sail.

Understanding shape

Rosie's farm

• Visualise and use everyday language to describe the position of objects and direction and distance when moving them

Setting up the activity (whole class or small groups)

As a group, decide how to stick down the picture cards on the large sheet of paper to make a simple map of Rosie's farm. Children do not need to keep to the layout in the story.

Together agree where to add paths to this map and draw them in. Keep this simple.

Next, talk about how maps are rather like what a bird sees when it looks down on a landscape. Get the children to stand up and look down on the map.

They then draw their own version of this map on A4 paper, keeping it as similar as possible to the large shared map.

Photocopy the maps so that you have two of each one. (Having duplicates means that in the 'Development' it doesn't matter whether the maps match the original.)

Can you remember where Rosie goes on her walk?

Tell me where we should put another path.

Is the beehive closer to the fence or the pond?
Look at our map and decide.

Development (teacher-led groups)

Pairs of children play a barrier game. They each have a copy of the same map and an identical set of about 5 farm animals. They work back to back or with a barrier between them. They take turns to pick an animal and decide where to put it, telling their partner who duplicates what they have done.

When they have placed all the animals, they compare maps and see how accurately they copied each other.

Where is the goat? Is it next to the haystack or on top of it?

Can you tell me what you did?

How could you make this easier? Harder?

What you need

• Cards cut from resource sheet 1

• A2 and A4 paper

• Photocopies of maps produced in the setting-up activity

• Small-world farm animals

Useful vocabulary

problem, explain, record, order, position, direction, outside, inside, beside, next to, front, back, between, underneath, above, on top of, below, halfway, near, far, whole turn, half turn, quarter turn, right, left

Winding it down (whole class or small group)

Arrange the large version of the map so that the children can see it and put an animal by each landmark and a picture card of Rosie by her henhouse. It is Rosie's birthday, and she wants to take some birthday cake to each of her friends who live around the farm.

Ask the children to tell you how to move Rosie to each friend in turn to deliver the cake and ask them to specify the route.

Who does she visit first?

Which path does she take? Is it the one that goes to the windmill?

Where is she now? Where has she just been? Where will she go next?

> ### Can the children
> - tackle this problem?
> - use and understand the language of position and direction?
> - make maps that have most of/all the features of the original? And in approximately the correct positions?
>
> Make notes during the activity about how children tackle the problem, work with others and the vocabulary they use.

Making it easier

Use fewer landmarks and arrange them in a simple circle, with one path connecting them all.

Making it harder

Increase the number of landmarks: for example, have two ponds and three beehives. Expect the children's maps to be closer to the original.

Links to other stories

Handa's Surprise
Children make maps of Handa's journey to visit Akeyo.

The Three Little Pigs
Children make maps of the village where the pigs live.

Areas of learning

Understanding English, communication and languages

- Children choose their favourite picture from the book. They describe the things in the picture and say what they like about them.

- Go on a walk around the school, with half the children being Rosie and half being the fox. As you go, reinvent the story based on the circumstances of the school environment.

- Add speech bubbles to the story to show what the fox and Rosie are thinking at each stage of the story.

Scientific and technological understanding

- Discuss the different habitats that are shown in the pictures: pond, field, beehives ... Talk about which animals and plants you can find in each habitat.

- Visit a real farm. Find out what animals live there, what jobs the farmers do to care for the animals, how the farm changes during the seasons ...

- Set up a 'farmyard' for the floor robot. Plan a route that will take the robot, as Rosie, safely around the yard. Plan a route that will make the robot, as the fox, bump into various objects.

Human, social and environmental understanding

- Discuss how farms can provide local produce to residential areas. Talk about how this used to be the norm, and how nowadays supermarkets often bring in food from around the country and from abroad, and why they do this.

- Look at old-fashioned and modern farming methods for milking, harvesting crops, and so on.

- Look at the animals in the story. Talk about what animals need to be happy and healthy. Discuss how we can help look after animals in the local environment by disposing of rubbish safely.

- Discuss whether foxes are a danger to children or just to animals such as the hen. Might foxes even be frightened of children?

Understanding the arts and design

- Use natural and classroom materials to make a collage showing animals from the city farm or park.

- Look at the detailed pictures in the story: for example, a tree with every leaf showing. Get inspired to make a detailed picture of your environment.

- Design a scarecrow to keep birds away from a vegetable patch to stop them eating the seeds and leaves.

- Make musical bird scarers from cans/old saucepans tied to a long piece of string. Beat them with a stick to scare the birds.

- Sing songs and action rhymes about farms such as: 'The farmer's in his den', 'Old Macdonald', 'Oats and beans and barley grow'. Help children make up their own verses to their favourite song.

Understanding physical health and well-being

- Talk about dangers the children might meet when out walking on their own, like Rosie in the story. What can they do to keep safe? Make a poster showing safety advice and stick it up in the school hall.

- Play the traditional game of 'Duck, duck, goose', but change it to 'Hen, hen, fox'.

- Play 'Grandma's footsteps', with 'foxes' trying to creep up on 'hens' that have their backs turned.

Resource sheet 1

Kipper's Birthday

Measuring

Mick Inkpen's much-loved book tells the story of Kipper, a little dog who is getting ready to celebrate his birthday. The cake is made, the balloons are blown up, but where are his friends? Why do they arrive a day late?

This is the story to introduce when you have a spate of birthdays in the class. Use it to help children focus on birthdays and other celebrations, or toys and presents, or friendship.

Maths overview

Using and applying mathematics

- Show children a packet of biscuits. Record their estimates about how many they think are in the packet, then open the packet and compare the actual amount with the estimates.

- Kipper's friends are wrapping his presents and want gift boxes for presents that are hard to wrap such as a ball or a whistle. Can the children make boxes for these presents?

- Kipper is making sandwiches for the party, using white and brown bread and three different fillings. What are all the different sandwiches he could make?

- Work with the children to make a toy shop's price list, using pictures from a catalogue. If each child has 10p, what would they buy from the shop? How many toys could they afford? Will they get any change?

Counting and understanding number

- How old is Kipper? Show children cards cut from resource sheet 1 with cakes showing up to 12 candles. Children estimate the number, then count to check.

- Children make sandwiches for the party and cut them into halves. They record how many half sandwiches they get for 1, 2, 3, 4 and 5 rounds.

- Look at cards cut from resource sheet 2. Children make birthday cards similar to these for a shop, then make a shop display, showing the cards in order of age.

Handling data

- What month do most children have their birthdays? Discuss how to collect the necessary information and how to present their results.

- Children find out everybody's favourite sandwich fillings and present the results as a simple bar chart or pictogram. They use this information for planning a class tea party.

- Sort birthday cards freely, then sort them using diagrams and criteria. Children re-sort in their own way and make labels to explain their sorting.

- Children draw all sorts of balloons. Play 'Guess my balloon'. Put a scrap of paper under one of the balloon pictures, while children look away. Give clues to help children which is your chosen one: "My balloon is blue. It has a picture of an animal on it. It has a really long string."

Calculating

- Pose simple word problems about birthday candles, involving more/less and doubling/halving such as: "Tiger has 3 candles on his cake, because he is 3. Kipper needs double that many. How many candles does Kipper need?" and "Big Ted needs 5 candles. Little Ted needs 1 less candle. How many candles does Little Ted need?"

- Use the price list from the fourth activity in the *'Using and applying mathematics'* section in the role-play shop. Children visit the shop and buy two items. They write the prices as a number sentence, find the total and draw the coins next to the total, showing how they will pay.

- Children write a price list for cake ingredients such as 'cherries 2p each' and pose problems based on this. What if Kipper needs 3 cherries? What is a reliable way to find the total?

Knowing and using number facts

- Show children several cards cut from resource sheet 1 with cakes showing 2 candles. Help children count the candles in twos. Repeat with cakes showing 5 or 10 candles.

- Write out a cake recipe with numbers of ingredients listed: 2 spoons of flour, 4 cherries, 10 currants, 3 eggs, and so on. Kipper needs to make two cakes, so he must double the ingredients. Can the children help him work out the quantities needed?

Kipper's Birthday

Measuring

 Snapshot activities
See pages 74-75

 Close-up activity
See pages 76-77

Understanding shape

- Make envelopes for cards. Take some envelopes apart to look at how they are made; focus on overlaps which allow you to stick paper to paper. Can children use this idea for their envelopes?

- Children wrap presents (models made from linking cubes) for Kipper. Using one piece of paper, what is the largest present they can wrap? What is the easiest/hardest shape to wrap?

- Make a parcel for 'Pass the parcel'. How many layers does it have? How big does it get and what shape is the final parcel?

- Wrap up some 3D solids as presents and play a game of 'What am I?' Children feel a present and try to guess what shape it contains. They open the present to see if they are correct.

Measuring

Kipper's birthday cake

- Weigh objects, choosing and using suitable uniform non-standard or standard units and measuring instruments

What you need: Paper and pen, balance or cups, cooking equipment, ingredients for making a cake

Together, write a simple cake recipe with units of measurement such as cubes. Discuss how to measure the ingredients with a balance, then make the cake.

Or make birthday pancakes, which involves measuring liquid.

Weighing presents

- Estimate, weigh and compare objects, choosing and using suitable uniform non-standard units and measuring instruments

What you need: Three wrapped 'presents', balance, various non-standard units; 1 g and 10 g weights

Give the children three wrapped 'presents' (make sure that the largest present is not also the heaviest). Children look at and feel the presents and place them in order of estimated weight.

Discuss the importance of using uniform units and suitable measuring equipment. Provide a balance and a range of non-standard units such as fir cones, pebbles, cubes. Children choose units, weigh each present and record their results. They then order the presents by weight and compare this result with their initial estimates.

Making it easier

Write a cake recipe, using cups as units: for example, a full cup of flour, half a cup of currants … Children then make the cake.

Making it harder

Write a recipe, using standard units such as 100 g.

Making it easier

Compare only two presents.

Making it harder

Weigh and compare four or five presents. Use 1 g and 10 g weights. Record findings in a simple table.

A calendar month

• Use vocabulary related to time

What you need: Blank calendar pages; number line or track

Talk about why Kipper's friends came to his party a day late. Discuss how to use a calendar to fix a party date and how this can help avoid such confusions.

Show childen a blank calendar page for the current or next month. Agree the day of the week that the 1st falls on and write this in. Pass the page round the group; children take turns to write the next date in the correct place.

When the page is finished, everybody chooses a date they think Kipper should have his party. They say the date and the day of the week that day falls on.

Making it easier

Use a number line or track to support writing the dates.

Making it harder

Children complete their own calendar page.

Party drinks

• Estimate, measure, weigh and compare objects, choosing and using suitable uniform non-standard or standard units and measuring instruments

What you need: Litre jug and cups

Explain that Kipper needs enough drink for the party. He has a jug, but is not sure whether it holds enough drink for four people. Give children a litre jug and just one cup. Discuss with them how they can find out how many cupfuls the jug holds.

Making it easier

Provide enough cups so that children do not need to empty and refill the same cup.

Making it harder

Suppose everybody wants two drinks. Will the jug hold enough?

Measuring

Party hats

- Estimate, measure and compare objects, choosing and using suitable uniform non-standard units and measuring instruments

Setting up the activity (whole class on carpet)

The animals are going to a hat shop to buy party hats for Kipper's party.

Show children your party hat. Try it on the animals, discuss which ones it fits and establish the idea that different animals need different-sized hats. Talk about real hat shops where grown-ups go, and where hats are marked with different sizes. Give each pair some paper strips of various lengths and establish a method of making a hat for their animal by sticking the ends together with no overlap.

Development (pairs and whole class)

Children measure their strips of paper with cubes or other units and write approximately how many units long it is on each one, then turn it into a hat. They decorate the hats and put them in the 'hat shop' (designate a place for this, such as a low table).

Do the cubes need to be close together or spaced out when you measure?

Is that hat a good fit? Or is it too loose/tight?

How could you tell or show someone else what you have done?

Winding it down (whole class)

As a class, take each animal to the shop in turn. The shopkeeper asks the animal if they know their hat size and helps them find a hat to fit. The shopkeeper records the size (in units) by the animal's name so that next time they come to the shop, they will know what size of hat to look for.

When all the animals are fitted out, look at the records and discuss the activity.

Do you think the koala needs a big hat? What size do you estimate that it needs?

If there is no hat size 12 to fit the duck, what can we do about it?

How many hats did we make in size 10?

Which animals needed the largest hat? The smallest hat?

What you need

- Stuffed animals of various sizes
- A simple party hat, based on a thick band of paper to fit around the head
- Paper strips of varying lengths
- Sticky tape
- Linking cubes, short sticks or square tiles
- Materials for decorating hats

Useful vocabulary

explain, compare, measure, unit, length, size, long, short, longer/longest, shorter/shortest, large, small, how many?

What did you find easy and hard about the task?
Would you do anything differently next time?

Can the children

• measure accurately with non-standard but uniform units?

• recognise the benefit of using uniform units as opposed to, for example, sticks of differing lengths?

• use mathematical language (longer than, shorter than, the same length as, close to, nearly) to compare the lengths of the strips directly?

• describe how they made the hats?

Make notes during the activity about how children tackle the problem, work with others and the vocabulary they use.

Making it easier

Have strips of suitable lengths prepared, but do not measure with units. Children find a strip to match each teddy and turn them into hats. Talk about the length of the strips and whether any are too long or too short.

Making it harder

Show children how to use a ruler to measure the strips of paper to the nearest centimetre.

Links to other stories

Handa's Surprise
Children make headbands for themselves to support a basket like Handa has on her head.

Sleeping Beauty
Children make and decorate cone-shaped fairy hats.

Areas of learning

Understanding English, communication and languages

- Plan a party for the class: write invitations, a party menu and a shopping list.

- Set up a party for one of the dolls in the role-play area. Children make invitations and a birthday banner.

- Look at recipe books, then write out your own instructions for making party food.

- Make a class book of favourite party foods. Talk about the front cover, pictures, text, contents page and index.

- Think about behaviour at parties. Can the children describe a polite guest and a rude guest? Explore this through role play.

- Why did Kipper's friends not come to his party? Talk about misunderstandings and how easily they can happen. How did Kipper feel? What did he think when no one came? How did he feel the next day when they arrived?

Scientific and technological understanding

- Make a cake. Discuss how the ingredients mix together; what happens when the cake is put in the oven; how the cake changes; what makes it rise …

- Take photographs of the stages of making a cake and use them to illustrate a recipe.

- Make jelly and look at the changes in consistency during the process. Use a range of moulds and talk about what happens when you tip out the jelly.

- Look at balloons. What happens when we blow into them? Let the air out? Why do balloons burst? Sort objects into things that would/would not burst a balloon and test a few of them.

- Use the computer to write a 'thank you' letter from Kipper to one of his friends.

- Wrap 'presents' using a range of papers and materials. Which materials are easy to use and which aren't?

Outdoor opportunities

Decorate a corner of the outdoor area with balloons and discuss how to stop them blowing away.

Human, social and environmental understanding

- Look at birthday cards for people of different ages. Talk about who in the children's families could be each age. Discuss how they themselves expect to change as they grow older.

- Sequence pictures onto a timeline: baby, toddler, schoolchild, teenager, adult and pensioner.

- Recount special events and celebrations. Which ones have special memories attached?

- Talk about which shops in your local area the children would visit to get items for a party.

Understanding the arts and design

- Make wrapping paper. Look at some examples and print repeating patterns with sponges or other objects such as cotton reels, car wheels, and so on.

- Use balloons for papier-mâché modelling: mix torn-up newspaper with PVA glue and cover the balloon with this mix. When dry, pop the balloon and decorate. Use as permanent balloons which won't deflate.

- Sing celebratory songs such as 'Happy birthday'.

- Make party hats or party bags. Look at some examples and discuss how to construct them, the best materials to use, and how to join the materials together.

Understanding physical health and well-being

- Talk about party food and healthy and unhealthy options. Plan a healthy menu for a party. Discuss hygiene in relation to preparing the food.

- Play some traditional party games.

- Use balloons as a stimulus for dance. Children make up simple dance sequences that show a balloon being blown up, travelling through the air and popping.

Resource sheet 1

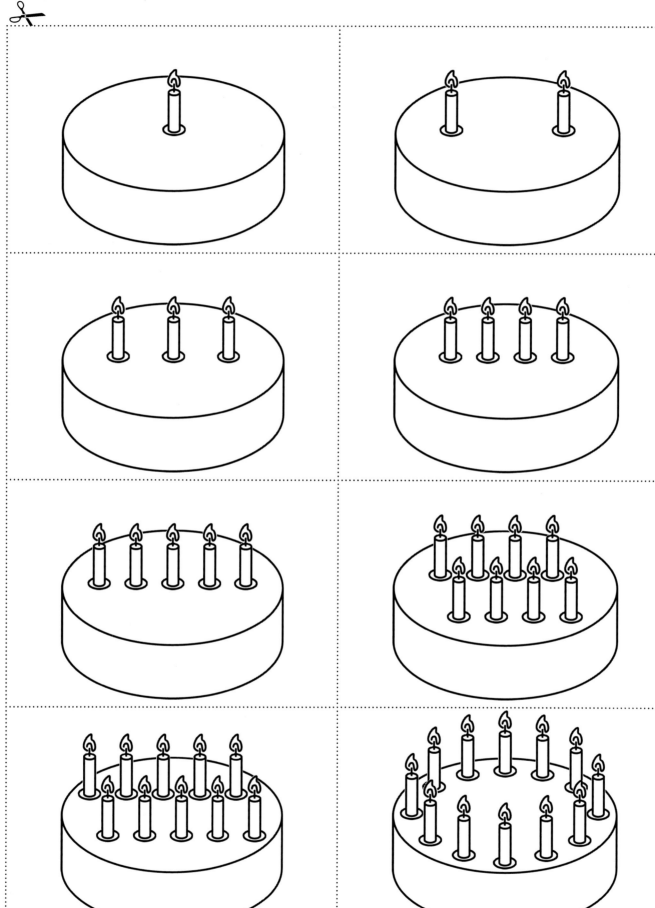

Handda's Surprise

Handling data

Eileen Browne's *Handa's Surprise* is set in Kenya: a girl called Handa packs a basket of fruit to take to her friend Akeyo's village. On her way, she encounters animals who steal her fruit until the basket is almost empty. The final animal, a goat, bumps into a tree, filling her basket with tangerines. Akeyo is overjoyed when Handa arrives with a basket full of tangerines – her favourite fruit.

Use this story as part of your work on 'Our world'. Alternatively, focus on it when discussing healthy eating or growing food. Or surprise your class by having a topic all about surprises!

Maths overview

Using and applying mathematics

- The pineapple in Handa's basket cost her 7p. What coins might she have used to pay for it?

- Handa needs help to pack her basket. How can children find out which fruits are heaviest (they need to be at the bottom of the basket) and which are lighter (they need to be at the top)? What equipment will they need? Ask children to record their findings.

- Start a pattern using plastic animals or animal cards cut from resource sheet 1: giraffe, goat, goat, giraffe, goat, goat ... Work as a class to describe and continue the pattern. Make some deliberate mistakes for the children to spot. Children then make up their own patterns.

Counting and understanding number

- Set up five bowls with real or pretend fruit. Children count the fruits in each bowl, make labels showing the number of fruits and put the bowls in order.

- Cut some apples into halves and quarters. How many halves or quarters make a whole?

- Set up two 'fields' in different parts of the room, with a different number of toy animals in each (or use cards cut from resource sheet 1). Compare the fields and talk about how to find out which has more animals, using a number line or track as appropriate. Progress to replacing animals with number cards and discuss how to compare quantities now.

Measuring

- Handa is going to visit another friend. She is taking 5 apples (or 8 oranges or whatever fruit you have available). Can the children find the best container to hold the fruit?

- Guess whether the peach or the banana weighs more. Check, using a balance.

- Guess whether the apple in Handa's village or the banana in Akeyo's weighs more. Discuss with children how to find out without making a direct comparison. Move towards the idea of weighing each one, using cubes, and finding out which uses most cubes.

Knowing and using number facts

- Handa has 10 pieces of fruit. How many different ways could she put them into two baskets?

- Each child in a group draws two fruits. Work out how many pieces of fruit there are altogether by counting in twos.

- Fill a basket with 10 fruits (or coloured counters). Children count back in ones as each animal removes a piece of fruit. Extend to a basket with 20 or 30 fruits, from which animals remove two, five or 10 pieces of fruit at a time.

Calculating

- Fill a basket with five fruits (or coloured counters). Roll a dice and choose whether to add that many fruits or remove them from the basket. Keep track of the running total by working it out mentally, with fingers or a number line, but don't count the fruits until the end. When you decide to stop, count the fruits and see if the totals match.

- Each child has 10 pieces of play fruit in a bowl (or use cards cut from resource sheet 2). The group shares two dice, one with pictures of animals and the other with numbers to 6. Children roll both dice to find out how many pieces of fruit an animal takes and tell the group what has happened: "I had 10 fruits in my basket, and the giraffe stole 4 of them." They remove that many fruits and quickly record the number stolen. When everybody has told their story, each child writes a subtraction sentence to match their story.

10 - 4 = 6

- Spread out some number cards face down on the table.

Children choose two cards (one card for each basket), say the number and put in that many pieces of fruit. They find the total and write the matching addition sentence.

- Show children a basket with a number of tangerines divisible by the number of children. Ask them to share the fruit between them. How many do they have each? What other numbers of tangerines could the children share fairly?

Handa's Surprise

Handling data

Snapshot activities
See pages 86-87

Close-up activity
See pages 88-89

Understanding shape

- Look at the fruits in Handa's basket (or in a real basket of fruit). Choose one in secret and describe it using size and shape words, but no names of fruit and colour words. Can children work out which one you are thinking of? Children then take turns to do the same.

- Make some crossing paths on the floor with chalk or masking tape. Put various fruits at places along the paths. Instruct children which paths to choose in order to collect the fruits, using the language of left and right, and quarter, half and whole turns: "Turn left through a quarter turn. Walk straight ahead. Stop and collect the pear."

- You need a large 5 by 5 grid. Put fruits in some of the squares and colour the sides of the grid in different colours. Instruct children to move a play person around the grid to collect the fruit: "Move 2 squares towards the red side. Stop. Move one square towards the yellow side. You have won a lemon!"

Outdoor opportunities

Make a large map on the floor of the route Handa took from her village to Akeyo's village. Children take on the roles of the animals and steal fruit as a child playing Handa moves across the map to visit Akeyo. Talk about where each animal is standing or sitting.

Handling data

Tasting fruit

- Answer a question by recording information
- Present outcomes using practical resources

What you need:
Two or three different fruits

Children taste two or three different fruits. Talk about a way they can record which fruits people liked and did not like and help the children carry out their ideas. Discuss the problems that arise: for example, if they place pictures of fruits in 'like' or 'dislike' sorting rings, people may assess fruits differently, so the same fruit gets

put in both rings. Thinking about such problems is useful, so encourage children as much as possible to try and find solutions themselves.

Sorting animals

- Sort objects into groups according to a given criterion
- Suggest a different criterion for grouping the same objects

What you need: Cards cut from resource sheet 1 or toy African animals; two sorting rings or bowls

Give children pictures of animals cut from resource sheet 1 or toy African animals. Explain that all the animals live in Africa, but have other similarities and differences. Discuss some of these.

Children sort the animals according to a given criterion such as 'feathers/no feathers' or 'has a long neck/does not have a long neck'. Discuss with the children any animals they are not sure about and encourage them to make their own decisions.

Ask the children to sort the animals in their own way and help them make labels for the sets. Help them talk about how they chose their criteria and ask them to describe both sets, using the word 'no' or 'not' as appropriate.

Making it easier

Children taste only one kind of fruit and discuss how to record their reactions.

Making it harder

Expect children to devise questions which require them to interrogate their graph or chart. Questions could include: "Which fruit did most people like?"; "How many more liked … than …?"; "Which was the least popular fruit?"

Making it easier

Provide two sorting rings or two bowls to encourage children to sort into two sets. Talk with them as they sort, helping them express their ideas and questions.

Making it harder

Challenge children to sort by two criteria, using a Carroll diagram with four sections: for example, *long neck, not a long neck, yellow, not yellow.*

Choosing fruit

- Sort objects into groups according to a given criterion
- Suggest a different criterion for grouping the same objects

What you need: Basket, cards cut from resource sheet 2; real fruit, sets of different objects

Children sit in a circle on the carpet with a basket in the middle. Give each child a fruit card cut from resource sheet 2. Take on the role of Handa, choosing fruit for her basket. Handa has a criterion in mind, such as fruits that need to be peeled or round fruits, but doesn't say what this is. Each child in turn asks: "Can my fruit go into your basket?", and Handa replies: "Yes" or "No". If the answer is 'yes', the child puts their fruit in the basket. Together, the children try to work out Handa's criterion. When they have found the criterion, one of the children takes on the role of Handa.

Picnic basket

- Answer a question by recording information in lists and tables

What you need: Selection of food items

Present children with a selection of foods: empty packets, real food, pictures … Pose a question for them to investigate: "Which of these foods would our class choose to pack in a basket to take on a picnic?"

Talk to the children about how they can find the answer and work with them to make a data-collection sheet such as a table or tally chart. Children use this to collect information from their classmates. Children report back to the class, showing their chart and discussing their findings. Together, identify the most popular items to pack in a basket.

Making it easier

Use real fruits.

Making it harder

Children are likely to choose to make this harder of their own accord by choosing 'difficult' criteria. You can also suggest they play the game with other sets of objects such as building blocks or coins.

Making it easier

Expect to give children substantial support in making and using a table or tally chart. Start off the recording with them in order to provide a model to scaffold their recording.

Making it harder

Children record their findings as a block graph.

Handling data

Favourite fruits

- Answer a question by recording information in lists and tables
- Present outcomes, using practical resources, pictures, block graphs or pictograms

Setting up the activity (whole class)

Talk about Akeyo's favourite fruit being tangerines. If Handa was going to bring a basket of fruit to the class, what should she bring? What kind of fruit is the class's favourite?

Children talk in pairs about how they will find out this information: what questions they need to ask, and how they will collect the information.

How will you make sure you ask everybody just once? And not leave anyone out?

Gather in children's ideas and help them shape the idea of a simple table or tally chart. Explain that once they have collected the information on this, you will help them display it on a block graph to send to Handa; this will show her what to bring the class.

Development (whole class)

Invite one or more pairs to use a simple table or tally chart to collect information about each child's favourite fruit. This need not be restricted to fruit on the picture cards, as you can quickly sketch other fruits on blank cards, as necessary.

Once the children have collected the information, share it with the class. Together, work out how many children liked each kind of fruit. Move on to displaying this information as a human block graph.

Put large pictures of the fruit on the carpet and ask children to line up behind their favourite fruit. Take a photo of the children and talk about how they have created a human block graph.

Together, count the children in each line and compare the results to find out which fruit is the favourite.

How many more children prefer oranges to bananas?

Do fewer people like apples or grapes?

What is the most (or least) popular fruit in the class?

What can you tell me about the human block graph we made?

What you need

- Enlarged pictures of fruit (resource sheet 2)
- Blank cards on which to sketch other fruits
- Camera
- Basket with real fruit (optional)
- Squared paper
- Data-handling program (optional)

Useful vocabulary

represent, interpret, tally, block graph, information, table, most/least popular, how many?, how many more is … than …?, how many fewer is … than …?

Winding it down (whole class or small group)

The children make a paper block graph. Each child draws a picture of their face and sticks it above a picture of their favourite fruit on a large piece of paper.

Interrogate the picture block graph again.

Ask children to think of a title for the block graph, to write at the top before sending it to Handa.

What can you tell me about the real block graph we have made?

Does it show the same information as the human block graph? How can we check?

Do fewer people like apples than grapes on this graph as well?

Are bananas still the most popular fruit in the class?

If possible, arrange that a basket of their favourite fruit arrives the following day as a gift from Handa.

Can the children

- share ideas about how to collect the information and represent it?

- find a way to record information accurately and systematically?

- find out the answer to the question using the block graphs created by the class?

- understand how to construct a simple block graph or offer support to those who do not understand?

Make notes during the activity about how children tackle the problem, work with others and the vocabulary they use.

Making it easier

Use simple questions to support children's interpretation of the chart, such as: "How many children like apples?"; "Can you count how many like strawberries?"; "Show me with your fingers how many people like pineapple."

Making it harder

Children use squared paper to explore making their own block graphs. They can draw pictures of the fruit along the bottom of the paper and colour the appropriate number of blocks above.

Children could also use a data-handling program to create their own block graph. Children then use their graphs to ask each other questions, as modelled by an adult.

Links to other stories

The Three Little Pigs
In what type of home would children in the class choose to live? Collect the information and present it as a block graph.

Kipper's Birthday
How old are children in the class? What is a good way to present this information?

Areas of learning

Understanding English, communication and languages

- Children write an invitation from Akeyo asking Handa to visit her village.
- Children write a card from Akeyo, thanking Handa for the tangerines.

- Children collaborate to write their own version of the story, set in England, with animals from their local area stealing the food in the basket.

- Talk about the surprise Handa gave Akeyo. Was it a nice surprise or a nasty one? Who exactly was surprised by the gift? How might the children surprise a friend or member of their family?

Scientific and technological understanding

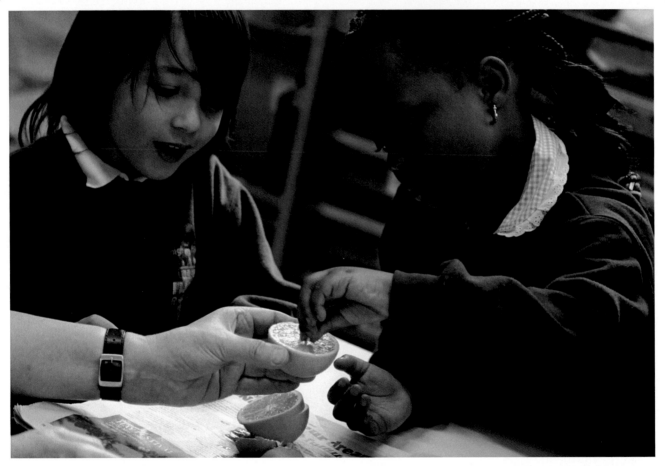

- Challenge the children to think of a waterproof covering for Handa's basket. Children test different materials and decide how to attach them to the basket.

- Suggest children use reference books to find out how the fruit in the story is grown: on trees, bushes, vines …

- Cut up some fruit; children try to identify the seeds. Discuss what these are like and how they differ.

- Together, taste some fruits and discuss the different textures, smells and tastes.

- Use clip art to insert pictures of the fruit or animals in the story into a word file and write captions or labels to accompany the pictures. Help children use the Internet or a CD-Rom to find out about animals that live in Africa.

Outdoor opportunities

Children explore how to move fruit from one side of the outdoor area to the other, using boxes, ropes, guttering …

Human, social and environmental understanding

- Set up a travel agency. Children research Kenyan lifestyles and customs and make a simple picture brochure or poster.

- Explore similarities and differences between the children's life and Handa's: clothes, climate, housing, animals, transport, food …

- Look at labels on fruit to find out where in the world it comes from. Try to sort fruits into those grown in the UK and those we have to import.

Understanding the arts and design

- Find out about Kenyan art on the Internet. Try batik, soapstone carving (try carving soap instead) or making face masks (look at pictures of traditional Kenyan face masks).

- Arrange a selection of the fruit from the story for still-life observational drawing, using pastels or charcoal. Cut the fruit in half and complete a second drawing.

- Make baskets. Cut out sections from a paper plate leaving the shape of the sun. Bend these 'rays' upright and weave wool or paper through to make the basket.

- Learn songs and rhymes about fruit and vegetables such as 'One potato, two potato'.

- Paint portraits of Handa or Akeyo.

Understanding physical health and well-being

- Children listen to African music and respond to it through movement.

- Set up an 'obstacle course' for Handa to travel along on her way to reach Akeyo's village. Represent obstacles such as rivers, hedges or fields of crops, using benches, tables, ropes, and so on. Ask children to balance a quoit or beanbag on their head instead of a basket and try to negotiate the course without dropping it.

- Discuss modes of transport. Is it better for you to walk or to travel by car or bus? Do you walk to visit friends, as Handa does?

- Discuss the contents of Handa's basket in terms of healthy eating. What might have been less healthy contents?

- Use fruits from the story to make a fruit salad. Talk about how to work hygienically. Ensure the safe use of tools when cutting the fruit.

Resource sheet 1

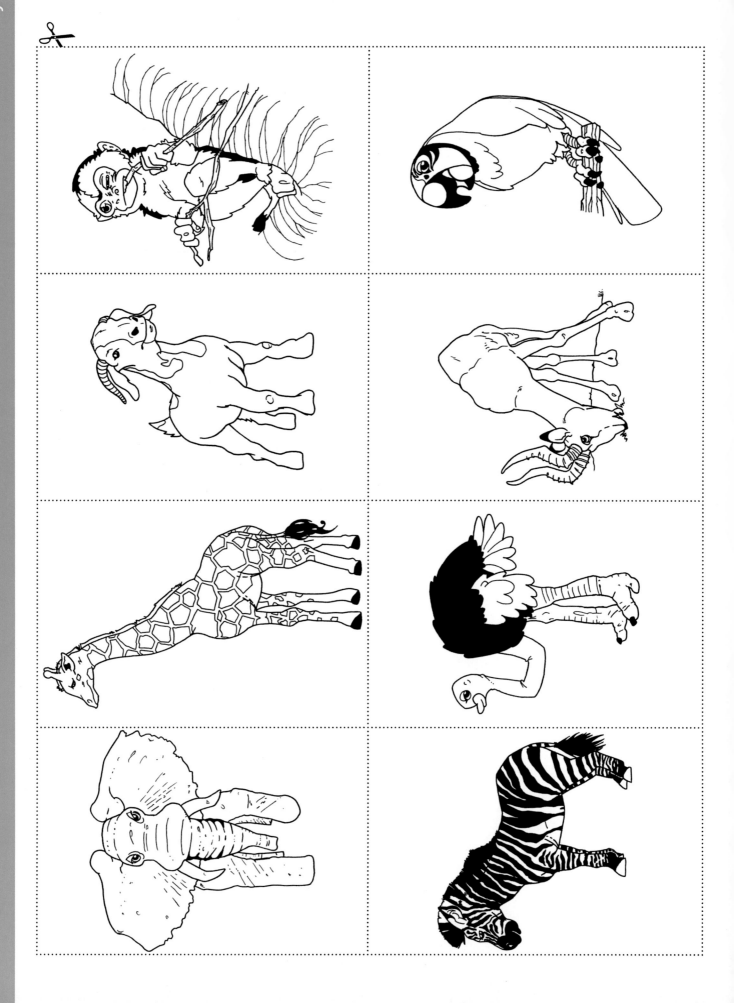

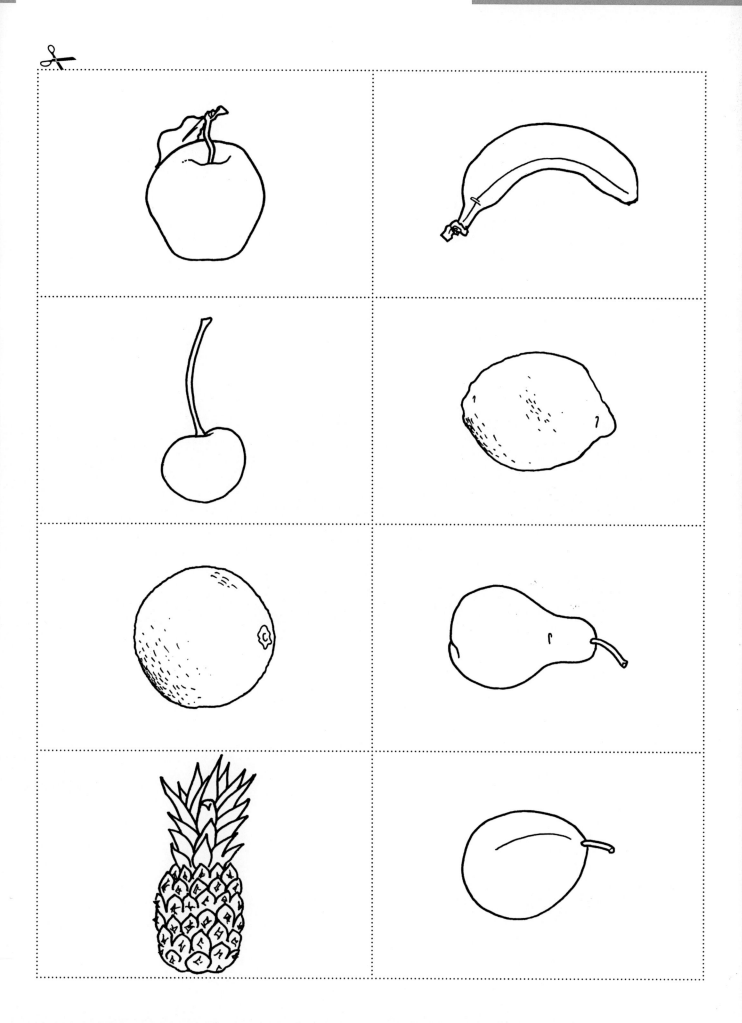